The Forgotten Chaucer Scholarship of Mary Eliza Haweis, 1848–1898

T0298367

The author of numerous books on Geoffrey Chaucer, the nineteenth-century scholar, Mary Eliza Haweis, has been largely erased from general histories of Chaucer studies. In her critical biography, Mary Flowers Braswell traces Haweis's career, bringing her out of obscurity and placing her contributions to Chaucer scholarship in the context of those of influential Chaucerians of the period such as Frederick James Furnivall, Walford Dakin Selby, and Walter Rye. Braswell draws on extensive archival research from a broad range of late-Victorian newspapers, journals, and society papers to weave a fascinating picture of Haweis's own life and work, which in quantity and quality rivaled that of her contemporaries. Haweis, we discover, corrected assumptions related to the Chaucer seal and texts, bringing her findings to the attention of the public in works such as *Chaucer for Schools*, the first textbook on the poet. Braswell also sheds light on the ways in which fashion, society, culture, art, and leisure activities intermingled with scholarship, archival recovery, museum work, editing, writing, and publishing in the late-Victorian middle and upper classes. Concluding with a discussion of Haweis's forgotten role as head of the Chaucer section for the National Home Reading Union, Braswell's book makes a strong case both for Haweis's influence as a Chaucer scholar and her importance as an educator in nineteenth-century Britain and the United States.

Mary Flowers Braswell is Professor Emerita of English at the University of Alabama at Birmingham, USA.

The Forgotten Chaucer Scholarship of Mary Eliza Haweis, 1848–1898

Mary Flowers Braswell

Routledge
Taylor & Francis Group

LONDON AND NEW YORK

First published 2017 by Routledge

2 Park Square, Milton Park, Abingdon, Oxfordshire OX14 4RN
52 Vanderbilt Avenue, New York, NY 10017

Routledge is an imprint of the Taylor & Francis Group, an informa business

First issued in paperback 2019

British Library Cataloguing in Publication Data
A catalogue record for this book is available from the British Library

Library of Congress Cataloging-in-Publication Data
Names: Braswell, Mary Flowers, 1943– author.
Title: The forgotten Chaucer scholarship of Mary Eliza Haweis (1848–98) / by Mary Flowers Braswell.
Description: Farnham, Surrey, UK, England : Ashgate Publishing Limited ; Burlington, VT : Ashgate Publishing Company, 2016. | Includes bibliographical references and index.
Identifiers: LCCN 2015045583 (print) | LCCN 2016015736 (ebook) | ISBN 9781472451712 (hardcover : alk. paper)
Subjects: LCSH: Haweis, Mary Eliza, 1848–1898. | Literary historians—England—Biography. | Medievalists—England—Biography. | Critics—England—Biography. | Women scholars—England—Biography. | Scholars—England—Biography. | Women educators—England—Biography. | Educators—England—Biography. | Haweis, Mary Eliza, 1848–1898—Knowledge—Literature. | Chaucer, Geoffrey, –1400—Influence.
Classification: LCC PR55.H39 B73 2016 (print) | LCC PR55.H39 (ebook) | DDC 821/.1—dc23
LC record available at https://lccn.loc.gov/2015045583

ISBN: 978-1-4724-5171-2 (hbk)
ISBN: 978-0-367-88091-0 (pbk)

Typeset in Times New Roman
by Apex CoVantage, LLC

As always, to John.

Contents

Figures

Figure I.1 Chaucer and the Pilgrims
Source: *Chaucer for Children.*

Introduction

> The mid-years of the nineteenth century established the terms of discourse for Chaucer criticism. To a surprising degree these early anonymous critics, rather than the great names of later Chaucer criticism, set the agenda for many popular, durable, pervasive ideas about Chaucer the writer and Chaucer the man.
>
> Carolyn P. Collette, "Chaucer and Victorian Medievalism: Culture and Society," *Poetica* (1989), 29–30

In 1876, the English publishing house of Chatto & Windus announced a unique Chaucer text. Not an edition per se, like those of Thomas Speght, Thomas Tyrwhitt, Thomas Wright, John Bell, and Richard Morris, it nevertheless referenced those editions and was quick to criticize sloppy or "incorrect" scholarship. Not exactly a child's book, it contained a "once upon a time" format and the promise of "wonderful stories" to come. Unlike the works of Cowden Clarke, Richard H. Horne, and Mary Seymour, this book contained a biography based on original documents, manuscript numbers, and collated texts, and other primary source material drawn from libraries and archives. The text was glossed, with extended footnotes, allowing readers to follow its author at work and form conclusions about the effectiveness of the analysis, and it assumed considerable previous knowledge from the reader. The list of referenced male scholars and their findings within its pages resounds like a roster from the Chaucer Society itself, an association the author was never invited to join. New discoveries, unpublished hypotheses, and echoes of salty academic squabbles fill the pages of this book. Unlike anything before it or since, it is the careful and accomplished work of Mary Eliza Joy Haweis.

My introduction to the work of Mrs. Haweis came curiously in February of 2001, when an unfamiliar editor of a Victorian encyclopedia emailed me to write on Haweis's *Chaucer for Children*. I had never encountered Haweis, and I wondered why, since she was apparently important enough to warrant an encyclopedia article on her own merit. I volunteered to write the article, but by that time the instigator had vanished into the murkiness of cyberspace from which she never returned. Intrigued, however, I ordered *Chaucer for Children* on interlibrary loan, but the handful of U.S. libraries that actually possessed it were not willing to send it. It was labeled "non-circulating," or "library use only," or "special collections," and was located in places too far away for me to travel to conveniently. The copy from SUNY at Albany was lost (they *had* been willing to loan), and Yale's available copy was missing as well. The University of British Columbia tantalizingly displayed the book on their website for the Arkley Collection's "Medieval Books for Children," but they, too, steadfastly refused to send it, to digitize it, or to photocopy it. Finally, by chance, the Atlanta-Fulton Public Library added its own holding of the text to the OCLC list and agreed to a short, nonrenewable loan. I gleefully photocopied all of it and sent it back posthaste. Years later, the book is available everywhere: used book stores, Google Books, print on demand, eBay; I have now acquired more copies than I could ever want. But that is now.

My weeks waiting for *Chaucer for Children*, however, had not been misspent. Instead, I had read all the juvenile Chaucer texts I could find, both ancient and modern. Amazon.com alone boasted fifty-three titles, including the more recent *Chaucer the Cat and the Animal Pilgrims* (2001); the delightful and unexpurgated *Chaucer's "Canterbury Tales"* (2007), retold and illustrated by Marcia Williams; and *Chaucer the Puppy's Favorite Place* (2012). Victorian authors had weighed in as well. In 1833, Charles Cowden Clarke had written *Tales for Chaucer Told for Young People*, which contained a selection of the poet's works in prose, and in 1841, Richard Henry Horne rendered a poetic translation, borrowing tales from Wordsworth, Leigh Hunt, and Elizabeth Barrett. In 1884, Mary Seymour had published a prose rendition called *Chaucer's Tales Simply Told*. These works had in common the simplicity of language, the bowdlerizing of texts, and a lack of significant critical apparatus with which to read the stories more deeply. All of the selections were "safe," unsophisticated. Nobody referenced Haweis.

I sought out modern-day scholars on the Victorian Chaucer, although these were rare. Most important are Carolyn P. Collette's "Chaucer and Victorian Medievalism: Culture and Society,"[1] Charlotte C. Morse's "Popularizing Chaucer in the Nineteenth Century,"[2] and Siân Echard's *Printing in the Middle Ages*. For Collette, Chaucer represented "preeminent Englishness" in the mid-nineteenth century, a means of voicing dissatisfaction with the present by placing it against the "somewhat idealized medieval past" (p. 116). Her concern is with the more popular writers who viewed Chaucer as a "child-poet," a "poet of the English countryside," and a "poet businessman." She argues that Chaucer, "distant in time, was yet organically connected to the nineteenth-century . . . common man" (p. 117). Morse contends that Charles Cowden Clarke (1787–1877) and John Saunders (1791–1895) (along with Charles Knight, a book publisher) were the "most active boosters of Chaucer's common readership before the university in the mid-1860s took over the care and promotion of Middle English language and literature, including Chaucer" (p. 99). Echard, who does mention Haweis, sees her Chaucer as moral and religious: even his merriest stories have a fair moral and he shows an "acute awareness of forms and canons."[3]

As recently as 2012, however, Christina Von Nolcken unearthed one William Thomas Stead (1849–1912), who published the works of several Romantic and Victorian writers as "penny dreadfuls." He also included *The Canterbury Tales*, with numerous alterations, hoping that his book would enable "thousands, to whom Chaucer has been but a *name* and a shadow, to become a benefactor and a friend." "This edition is not for students of Chaucer," he asserts, as "it will only make them wild and expose them to homicide. But they are few and feeble folk at best."[4] Like Rev. H. R. Haweis in his *Tales from Chaucer* (see Chapter 3), he felt he was exposing the poet to the masses: "While directed to all classes of reader, it was especially intended to equip the 'ordinary common Englishman, country yokel, or child of the slums' and even 'that village girl lurking with lads on her way to the well'."[5] These writers – Collette, Morse, and Stead – have in common a lack of any mention of Mary Eliza Haweis and her work, although Stead likely knew the Rev. Haweis's production of the *Tales*.

None of my reading prepared me for the book I would finally acquire.

Who was Mary Eliza Joy Haweis (1848–1898)? According to the *Dictionary of National Biography* (s.v.), she was known mainly as a connoisseur of woman's fashion, and in an undated manuscript I would go on to find in the University of British Columbia Archives,[6] she claims to have been "the first to draw attention to the artistic side and philosophy of Dress and House Decoration – by precept – & example." She was an artist, the daughter of subject and portrait painter Thomas Musgrove Joy, who exhibited his daughter's work when she was seven years old – about the time she taught herself to read – and who, by the time she was sixteen, had sold a small painting for her at the Royal Academy. Her earliest articles, published in *St. Paul's Magazine*, were on the subjects of beauty and dress and she illustrated them lavishly with accurate period sketches. In 1879 she published them collectively as *The Art of Beauty*, a book that established her as an authority for women; it was followed by another in the same vein, *The Art of Decoration*, in 1889. Haweis wrote on a wide range of subjects of interest to women: "Servants and Served," "Jewels and Dress," "Art in Christmas Decorations," and "Young Wives and Their Difficulties." Her "long articles" appeared in the *Times*, the *Spectator*, *Saturday Review*, *Contemporary Review*, *Nonconformist*, *Truth*, *Morning Post*, *Mayfair*, *Academy*, *Athenæum*, *Echo*, and *Daily News*. She wrote "many short clips for other venues and published passing comments in leaders & public lectures [which] assured [her] that the sympathy of the English and American public . . . all along attended [her] work." She was vice president of the Central National Society for Women's Suffrage and for the Maternity Society of England, superintendent of the Women's Temperance Association, and a member of the Society of Women Journalists and the Society of Authors. She published scathing articles against vivisection and the wearing of too-tight corsets that damaged the anatomy. She was touted as "a lady of gentle birth, from whom nothing more was expected than that [she] should be inconspicuous as [a] wife and mother, and she was the first ever to write professionally, with convincing scholarship and authority for *women*" (emphasis mine).[7] She also wrote cleverly and brilliantly on Chaucer.

At nineteen Mary Eliza married the Rev. Hugh Reginald Haweis, a flamboyant preacher, violinist, and writer who was educated at Trinity College, Cambridge. He counted among his acquaintances and friends many American dignitaries like

Figure I.2 Portrait of Mary Eliza Haweis with monogram
Source: Photographer unknown.

Henry Wadsworth Longfellow, Ralph Emerson, Oliver Wendell Holmes, Walt Whitman, and Mark Twain. He wrote about these authors at length in his two-volume series *Travel and Talk*. He was Lowell lecturer in Boston in 1885, and throughout much of his adult life he was rector at St. James's Church, Marylebone, London. He was editor of *Cassell's Magazine* and of the *Routledge World Library Series*, and he wrote the celebrated *Music and Morals* and a five-volume series on *Christ and Christianity*. Although stunted, mutton-chopped, and lame from an early fall from a horse, he was also eloquent and exceptionally talented. Alternately proud of his precocious wife and gravely jealous of her, he was unfaithful. He fathered at least one illegitimate child with a parishioner and was blackmailed by at least one other. He depleted both the family's funds and his wife's health in his frenzied and futile bid to retain his good reputation. She disinherited him before she died.

Mary Eliza's scholarship was considerable and unique; it also made Chaucer available to a broader spectrum of English society than did the work of any of

Figure I.3 Portrait of Rev. Hugh Reginald Haweis, W & D Downey, 57 & 61 Ebary Street, London

Source: Photographer unknown.

her contemporaries. Today she is completely forgotten. Male scholars, some of whom relied heavily on her work, never credited her. Against considerable odds, both personal and professional – and rare for a woman of her day – she conducted her research in archives: in the Exchequer, the British Museum, and the Public Records Office, to name a few. She pored over manuscript variants, wrote for a wide-reaching audience, and lectured on the latest Chaucer discoveries from a variety of disciplines. Not only did she host a lavishly "correct" Chaucer ball, for which she supplied her guests with accurate costume patterns, but she was also the first to point out Chaucer's significant use of puns in *The Canterbury Tales* and to deem his maxims worthy of independent study. She was the first to speculate that behind certain of the pilgrim portraits lurked actual persons whom Chaucer knew, and also that Thomas Chaucer was the son of John of Gaunt. She analyzed Geoffrey Chaucer's landscapes by means of Richard Liebreich's theory of optics as applied to J.M.W. Turner. She corrected the images on the Thomas Chaucer seal from manuscripts at the miscellanea of the Queen's Remembrancer, and she argued convincingly on the fate of the missing Chaucer portrait Harleian MS 4826 from the British Museum. Her recorded evidence, gleaned from manuscript rolls and records, is not always chronicled elsewhere. She adapted *The Miller's Tale* for children, and she wrote the first Chaucer textbook that went through seven editions, remained in print for forty-four years, and was used widely in schools in England and America. In the year of her death she "took charge" of the prestigious Chaucer course for the National Home Reading Union, and she developed a "new theory" of Chaucer, which although now generally accepted is not ascribed to her.

Haweis's work is a rich repository of materials on Chaucer activities during the last quarter of the nineteenth century. It teems with learned footnotes and reveals, more than single articles, notices, or editions, the workings of the male scholars who shaped the Chaucer legacy. It indicates an extraordinary mind at work, not only on medieval records newly discovered but also on discussions based on those records. Haweis was acutely aware of manuscripts and their variations; she knew which editors had used which copies and why. She knew who owned personal copies and refused to lend, and she demonstrated firsthand knowledge of Chaucer's previous editors and of their annotations. Her comments on what this man thought or that man encountered often read like notes taken during actual discourse. In many cases, this is what they were.

Soon after she died, Haweis and her Chaucer scholarship effectively disappeared from view, leaving her theories to be propounded unheralded by her mentor Frederick Furnivall, and to be echoed eerily throughout the realms of Chaucer scholarship today by writers who never knew her name. Her books, lectures, and articles were replaced by those of her better-known male colleagues who totally eclipsed her. But considering Victorian Chaucer without Haweis squarely at its center is to consider such scholarship incomplete. Her diaries were destroyed, mostly by her husband; her letters were scattered and lost. Resurrecting the academic Haweis was no easy task. So obscure is her Chaucer work that one British archivist, whose repository had none of the records I had hoped to find, helpfully suggested to me: "Maybe she kept her scholarship a secret. Maybe she didn't want anyone to know." But Haweis, in fact, wanted *everybody* to know, and she spent much of her life promoting her work. This study is an attempt to restore her to her rightful place in the Chaucer tradition.

> NB: "When one considers bibliographic references from the point of view of the author or the reader, the assumption is that the citations are accurate. Unfortunately, considerable evidence exists that such an assumption is questionable."
>
> James H. Sweetland, "Errors in Bibliographic
> Citations: A Continuing Problem," *Library*
> *Quarterly* 59 (1989): 291–304

Bibliographical citations had not been precisely worked out in nineteenth-century England, and anyone researching in this area must be fully aware of this fact. It was not clear to most Victorian scholars precisely what information must be given to the reader so that anyone attempting to follow a reference could actually do so. The list of common errors was long: "miscited page numbers [or no page numbers]," "incorrect and misleading journal titles, and wildly misspelled authors' names." The most frequent mistakes were in the "author's name (surname or first name/initial), followed by those in date, volume or pagination" (Sweetland, p. 292). Many writers did not read the original, while others wrote confidently about fictional works – works they themselves had planned to publish, but had not. "Zolton J. Lucas, for example, cited nonexistent papers of his own (some rejected for publication) in National Institutes of Health (NIH) grant applications. His excuse: he planned to publish but became too busy" (Sweetland, p. 299).

Notes

1 Carolyn P. Collette, "Chaucer and Victorian Medievalism: Culture and Society," *Poetica* 29–30 (1989): 115–125. Further citations in the text.
2 Charlotte C. Morse, "Popularizing Chaucer in the Nineteenth Century," *Chaucer Review* 38:2 (2003): 99–125. Further citations in the text.
3 Siân Echard, *Printing the Middle Ages* (Philadelphia: University of Pennsylvania Press, 2008), 141.
4 Christina Von Nolcken, "Penny Poet, or Chaucer and the 'Penny Dreadfuls'," *Chaucer Review* 47:1 (2012): 107–133.
5 Ibid., 113.
6 Haweis Family Sous Fonds MEH Box 1, Misc. Box 31 (UBC).
7 Anonymous, "Advisers to the Victorians," MEH 2A Biographical folder #3, Box 31 (UBC).

1   The beginnings

Research, the records,
and the boys' club

She was self-disciplined and with a brain nurtured upon medieval literature, stepping lightly over the *Idylls of the King* which most young women of her day were reading as a sure stepping-stone to Mr. Ruskin's vision of white lace and lilies. She had great courage. She went directly to the source of the Idylls – the *Morte d'Arthur*, and the poetry of the father of English verse, Geoffrey Chaucer, who found readers only among the more highly educated literary scholars of her time. . . . She could by-pass Elinor Glyn and Ouida: Professor Skeat and Dr. F. J. Furnivall were her latter-day heroes. They were unaccustomed to being regarded by any young women whatsoever and I think they liked it.

Stephen Haweis
("Spoiled Child," Columbia University Archives, Box 2, p. 263.)

By the year 1875 Chaucer studies were flourishing in England. The Early English Text Society, founded in 1864, had issued Alexander Ellis's work *On Early English Pronunciation* and Walter Skeat's edition of *Treatise on the Astrolabe*. The Chaucer Society, created in 1868 by F. J. Furnivall, had just produced *The Ryme-index to the Ellesmere MS* by Henry Crombie, who had also promised to index "all the names of people and places mentioned, and all the subjects treated and alluded to in the *Canterbury Tales*."[1] The *Six Parallel Text Edition of the Canterbury Tales* had appeared with rave reviews and Furnivall was feverishly producing literary notices of new Chaucer discoveries, praising Henry Bradshaw and Bernhard ten Brink, for "the best work at and for [the poet] that has been done since his death."[2] John Wesley Hales's publications on Chaucer and Shakespeare raised new questions about influence studies,[3] and William Minto's biography of Chaucer in *Characteristics of English Poets* was newly published and highly acclaimed.[4] Trewman's *Exeter Flying Post* proudly announced that Professor John Morley had arranged "many quaint works [of Chaucer and his contemporaries] copied from old manuscripts" in his *The Library of Literature*, Volume II,[5] while Ten Brink's *Chaucer: Studies on the History of the Development and on the Chronology of His Writings* was in press, awaiting publication by Trübner of Strasburg.

In addition, the *Life Records of Chaucer* had appeared in print, providing fresh and provocative avenues of research for scholars and critics, particularly with regard to the newly available manuscripts flooding the British Library and the

Public Records Office. Members of the Chaucer Society flocked to whatever was available to cast light on their poet. In his Introduction to the *Life Records*, Walford D. Selby declared emphatically:

> There are vast collections of records which remain to be examined; that they should have been left untouched can be hardly wondered at, if we consider the dubious chances of success, and the time which would be required to complete such a task. . . . Consequently an exhaustive search . . . should include every document falling within the period of Chaucer's life [and] can be the only means of making sure that we know all that can ever be known about him.[6]

As late as 2006, Mark W. Turner echoed Selby's distress discussing the need for a systematic study of Victorian periodicals and the near impossibility of using them for comprehensive research. One problem, notes Turner, is access:

> Despite the best efforts of microfilming, full runs of even the most significant periodicals are not often widely available in libraries around the world. Furthermore, the fragility of hard copies prevents them from widespread use in many cases; no doubt we have all had the worrying experience in our own research of the crumbling page.[7]

A combination of lost and decaying manuscripts did and does constitute a major hurdle. A primary focus of the Chaucer Society would be the study of the unprinted and crumbling manuscripts both from their repositories and in the hands of private owners.

In addition to manuscripts, Britains turned to a reexamination of Chaucer's tomb.[8] They restored it and debated its proper date. Mr. M. H. Bloxam had earlier revealed that the monument was neither from Chaucer's own time nor from the time of Nicholas Brigham, but was made up of stones "plucked" by Brigham from Powles Church in 1552 – "a second-hand monument."[9] A window was installed in Poet's Corner. It depicted the Canterbury pilgrims, the poet receiving a commission from Edward III, and some lines from "The Floure and the Leafe (then thought to have been Chaucer's work.[10]) The reviewer suggested that, since the window had been completed, the tomb "should be cleared of some of the disfigurements around it."[11] He did not elaborate.

For years, the Tabard Inn had been used as a background for plays and masques.[12] Newspapers published modernizations (often comic) of Chaucer's poetry, and racehorses were named in his honor. The poet was a source of pantomimes and plays. Mr. E. T. Smith created a production featuring Chaucer and his pilgrims, John of Gaunt, Friar Bacon, and "the fairies."[13] One "Miss Braddon" wrote a play dubbed *Griselda*, which was performed at the Princess Theatre in 1873.[14] In 1875, the Rev. Carl Horstman re-edited *The Prioress's Tale* so that the grain on the little martyr's tongue read "Alma Redemptoris Mater";[15] the Rev. Dr. Leary lectured on "The Religious Element in Chaucer's Poetry,";[16] and Miss Eva Gordon of Pixholme

worked at translating Dr. P. Lindner's essay on "Alliteration in Chaucer."[17] Among
the variety of academic flurry was Mrs. Mary Eliza Joy Haweis, who wrote in her
diary on March 5, 1876: "All /75 I was working hard at my Chaucer book."[18]

The "Chaucer book" was not Mary Eliza's first foray into the publishing world;
at twenty-eight, she was already well known. However, the writings for which she
was celebrated – articles and advice for women – would undercut her future academic aspirations. As an authority on taste and beauty from a very early age, she
advised women on how to dress and minimize their imperfections, choose furniture, and decorate their walls. This reputation stuck. No matter how she struggled
to broaden her position later in life, she would forever be celebrated as "one who
alternated the duties of mother and housekeeper with the study of dress and interior decoration."[19] Her three children were often paraded as models of her "new
look," something her daughter Hugolin seemed especially to have despised. However as one astute critic noted, "Haweis's achievement was in establishing the link
between the 'feminine' role of the home-maker and the previously 'masculine'
preserve of the authoritative critic."[20]

Her earliest article seems to have been the 1872 "Art of Beauty," published
in the *Eclectic Magazine of Foreign Literature, Science, and Art* when Haweis
was approximately twenty-two.[21] However, in her autobiography she states, "I
wrote articles on the Aesthetics of Dress, Pedigree of Dress, Conditions of Costume, & kindred matters – also some papers on housekeeping – in the foremost
Magazines . . . from about 1867 when I married, to the present time."[22] She also
claimed to have been "the first to draw attention to the artistic side & philosophy
of Dress and House Decoration." In 1873, she published "Dress, Hints to Ladies"
for *Saint Paul's Magazine*. From September 15 to December 29 she published a
series of fashionable weekly articles for *Harper's Bazaar*, including "The Pain of
Ugliness," "Imbecile Ornament," "What Stays Cost Us," "Low Dresses," "Our
Poor Feet," "Hair-Powder and Patches," and "The Function of a Head-Dress."
She acquired a devoted female following. Essays such as these ("grade B," she
called them) would sustain her financially through lean periods in her life when
her husband, who mesmerized church audiences with his violin playing and elfin
charm, squandered the family finances on his mistress.

Within the world of aesthetics, Haweis was considered a "scholar." She studied
costume and paintings in the South Kensington Museum. She read widely, examined closely the wardrobes of society women and men with whom she mingled,
and displayed the utmost distaste for women who dressed in period costume without understanding its historical form and function: "I daresay that great lady over
there with the lappet and pouch-like thing is not aware that it is a revival of serf
costume of Henry II's time and is really a badge of servitude."[23] She confidently
asserted her authority in the domestic arena. But Haweis obviously had in mind
more lofty, academic goals than teaching society women how to dress, and for
these she needed to acquire specialized tools and cultivate a different audience.
Mark Taylor notes that Haweis had a "broad interest in art and decoration [which]
was matched by meticulous research. She saw connections between all sides of a

social and political issue, so that her apparent vacillations [were] simply proof of open-minded[ness] and tolerance."[24] Her productions ran the gamut from lectures on vivisection and too-tight shoes to book binding, sketching, and monogramming. She created Christmas cards, illustrated her husband's books, debated the merits of the best medieval manuscripts, and tested the limits of contemporary Chaucer scholarship.

She had no formal education, a fact that would prejudice her academic expertise among the "scholars." Having learned to read by "copying letters out of the newspapers," she received "practically no regular education other than what she picked up in her father's studio by reading the *Mirror of Literature, Amusement and Instruction.*"[25] Haweis touted her singularity, noting proudly in her autobiography that "there [has been] no example of literary taste in the family since the celebrated 'Sprat, Bishop of Rochester, an ancestor on my mother's side.'"[26] Her "textbook" was the British Museum and her remaining notebooks reveal just how closely she studied it.[27] They contain long, technical passages on Mohammed, gleaned from *Chamber's Encyclopedia.* She had read carefully *Njal's Saga*, a thirteenth-century account of a fifty-year-old blood feud, and analyzed it thoroughly, remarking on the lack of sympathy displayed by the author toward the physical suffering of his characters. On March 26, 1875, she attended an exhibition at the museum hosted by the painter and sculptor George Frederic Watts and recounted a conversation that the two had had about the art critic Ruskin and his dislike of Michelangelo and of Raphael's *Sistine Madonna.* They discussed as well the carving of slight muscles in sculptures and the strength that such small strokes produced – "The slighter the curve the greater the circle it is a section of." ("This is a splendid idea – and throws light on many things – the curves and sweeps of medieval figures, among others.") Haweis recounted her own comments as well as those of Watts, and it is clear that the twenty-seven-year-old woman could hold her own with the master. She added to her diary a list of court hands and their descriptions and ended in the middle of a sentence on broken engagements.

Mary Eliza contrasts sharply with her younger female contemporaries, Mary Bateson (1865–1906) and Caroline Spurgeon (1869–1942), who had strong academic ties and were recognized as scholars during their lifetimes. Bateson's father was the master of Saint James's College in Cambridge, where she attended the Misses Thornton's School. She also studied at the Institut Friedlaender in Germany, simultaneously teaching classes in German. She received a "certificate" at Newnham College, where her essay, "Monastic Civilization in the Fens" won her a first prize in history. Bateson was the only woman formally to be mentored by F. W. Maitland, Downing Professor at Cambridge, from whom she learned to edit, producing volumes for the Selden Society. When her two-volume edition of *Borough Customs* appeared, for which she is best known, he proudly heralded it as "not for the general reader," but only for a "few students of history," and he predicted that it would take its place beside *The History of the Exchequer* and *The History of Tithes.* Upon her death he wrote, "I do not know the *man* [emphasis mine] who both could and would have done so much and so well."[28] For Maitland,

Bateson had never stooped to write anything for the general reader. A woman of independent means, she devoted her brief life to medieval scholarship.[29]

Caroline Spurgeon, an only child born to an upper-middle-class family, was the "first proper and fully accepted woman professor of English studies and the first fully accepted woman professor in England in general."[30] She completed her doctorate summa cum laude at the University of Zurich with the dissertation *Chaucer devant la critique en Angleterre et en France depuis son temps jusqu'à nos jours*. She taught at the University of London, eventually becoming Hildred Carlisle Endowed Professor. She is most famous for her *Five Hundred Years of Chaucer Criticism and Allusion*, undertaken at the instigation of Furnivall, and is remembered for moving English studies away from philology and toward literature. She was published by the university presses at Cambridge and Oxford, and she edited *Richard Brathwait's Comments Upon Chaucer's Tales of the Miller and the Wife of Bath* in 1901 for the Chaucer Society.

Haweis had no scholarly publishers and no prestigious academic affiliations. Her most celebrated teaching assignment seems to have been the Chaucer course at the National Home Reading Union (see Chapter 5). Still, she managed to publish numerous books and articles, sometimes under extreme difficulties. The preparation for her own scholarship was of an entirely different sort.

Although Haweis, unlike Bateson and Spurgeon, had no access to university libraries, by the last quarter of the nineteenth century women regularly used the British Museum Reading Room for research. No women were employed in the museum except as housemaids or attendants in the ladies' rooms. In July 1894, Dr. Richard Garnett, former superintendent, remarked that "the proportion of women readers during my time [1851–1899] was from 10 to 20 percent. The ladies, as a rule, were very estimable readers, who had some definite object, and did not abuse the use of the room."[31] On October 14, 1872, Haweis applied for a ticket. She was number 4509 during the year 1872 and the fourth person to petition on that particular day. Applicants were required to ask in writing to the Director, "specifying the *particular purpose* for which they [sought] admission." According to the British Museum Signature of Readers, every application had to be accompanied

> by a written recommendation by a householder . . . who must also be a person of recognized position . . . with *personal knowledge* of the applicant . . . certifying that he or she [would] make proper use of the Reading Room.

In 1872 Haweis signed her name under the words "I have read the 'Direction respecting the Reading Room' and I declare I am not under twenty-one years of age."[32] All forms before the period of 1890 have been destroyed; we cannot know who recommended her or what her project was. Perhaps the Rev. Haweis signed her in. Subsequent evidence suggests, however, that her intermediary was Furnivall and that the project was her first book on Chaucer.

The British Library and its confines served as an academy for the self-taught woman, and she eagerly savored its offerings. Most of Haweis's diaries have been lost or were destroyed by her husband upon her death, but those that remain contain entries detailing very precisely with exhibits on ancient ornaments, objects of furniture, medieval painted glass, Assyrian bas-reliefs, and on and on. In *Chaucer for Children*, she included an illustration of "Dorigen and Aurelius in the Garden," where the husband and wife are playing chess with pieces that are clearly the Lewis Chessmen that the British Museum had acquired sometime between November 1831 and January 1832.[33] She took copious notes from exhibits, and while her observations are reflected in the *Art of Decoration* (1889), *The Art of Dress* (1879), and *The Art of Beauty* (1879), all of which she illustrated herself, such information also figures prominently in her writings on Chaucer's colors and medieval household furnishings, as well as in scholarly footnotes to her texts. The academic bibliographies contained in all of Haweis's works (those to which various reviewers would object) can be explained in part by the 20,000-plus volumes available to her from the British Library.

Equally important for our purposes, however, is that the repositories and reading rooms in the British Library (and in the Public Record Office as well) served as a kind of informal seminar setting, loosely attended by Haweis and a coterie of male friends who would thrive on her ideas and subsequently attain a level of scholarly renown. There are no official logs of these sessions, but Furnivall, Walter Rye, Emanuel Deutch, Walford D. Selby, and John Richard Green appear regularly in her publications and in her diary entries. It is obvious that she turned to them for assistance (*and* that they turned to her); that such persons were more than casually aware of each other's opinions and projects; and that much late nineteenth-century Chaucer scholarship was formulated under the blue, cream, and gold dome of the British Library ceiling.

> Their sense of a common purpose, their unity against those they felt undermined their social intercourse as well as intellectual and institutional closeness – all . . . are factors which gave [them] shape and definition. . . . Collaboration, citation of one another's works and informal communication [are] seen as tangible evidence of their existence.[34]

Additionally, their jovial repartee and the sometimes heated arguments are reflected in journals like the *Athenæum*, the *Manchester Times*, or in the prefaces to the EETS and the Chaucer Society editions.

Such groups are referred to in the scientific communities as "invisible colleges"[35] and reflect common ties based on common research interests. Smith points out the lack of critical attention paid to these scholarly nineteenth-century social gatherings, noting that such a forum appealed largely to males, engaged in archival work: "Professionals claimed that the search for historical truth in the seminar gave birth to a new community based on an agreement to find the authentic or real past."[36] Gatherings like these were especially popular among individuals who worked in archives, and they tended to proliferate when some new knowledge was developing rapidly. Philippa Levine argues that a key element of the methodology for such seminars was the emphasis on "the status of the text as the key source of historical investigation."[37] According to Levine, archival research had, by the turn of the century, become the sine qua non of the professional. It was from this belief in the verification through original sources that English empiricism derived its strength. "The reliance of ancient history on commentary . . . added further weight to the claims of the modern historians who could point to the pipe rolls and inquisitions post mortem that were becoming their stock in trade. Literary history receded and textually based accounts took precedence over form."[38] The importance of a gathering of such scholars, Chaucer text in one hand and plea and memoranda roll in the other – working simultaneously with both external and internal evidence – has been overlooked by critics, but it is crucial for an understanding of Haweis and for providing insight into late nineteenth-century scholars.

In England, this "scientific/literary" research was stimulated by scores of documents, largely medieval, being funneled into the archives where Haweis worked. Some of these were from private donors: for example, in 1871 the *Derby Mercury* noted that the collection donated by the Marquis of Salisbury contained "a fine and rare copy of Gower's *Vox Clamantis* and that the Marquis of Bath had donated works by Wycliff, as well as poems by Chaucer and Lydgate."[39] Such privately owned materials would have been stored safely. Most of the material, however, had been retrieved from places where it should never have been stashed. Accounts of the Public Records Office records – their destruction, their preservation, their large and unwieldy numbers – are vividly described in the local newspapers.

Individuals who had come to study witnessed cartloads of documents rumbling into repositories from who knows where; they saw the careless handling of priceless works. They understood – as we can never do from reading the secondary sources of modern critics, based on the secondary sources of other modern critics – the precarious nature of what little remained to investigate. They observed history in the process of being made and in the process of destruction. An anonymous deputy keeper of the archives wrote in his 1866 annual report that certain ancient records, kept in the Tower of London, were subjected not only to "fire and sword" but also to "water moths canker dust cobwebs [sic]."[40] He recalled the Miscellaneous Records of the Queen's Remembrancer, deposited in sheds in the King's Mews:

> [they contain] 4,186 cubic feet of archives, all damp, and covered with the dust of centuries. Some were in a state of inseparable adhesion to the stone walls. There were numerous fragments, which had only just escaped entire consumption by vermin, and many were in the last stage of putrefaction. Decay and damp had rendered a large quantity so fragile as hardly to admit of being touched; others, particularly in the form of rolls, were so coagulated together that they could not be uncoiled.

Ravenous predators scavenged the stacks:

> Six or seven perfect skeletons of rats were found embedded [in the manuscripts] (one of which is still preserved in the office as a curiosity) and bones

of these vermin were generally distributed throughout the mass; and, besides furnishing a charnel house for the dead, during the first removal of these national records a dog was employed in hunting the live rats which were thus disturbed from their nests.[41]

In 1882, for an article entitled "More News of Geoffrey Chaucer," Haweis echoed the same concern:

[A few years ago] a forgotten heap of parchments . . . was dug out of the cellar in King's Mews . . . intact without, however dusty with the dust of ages, but inwardly nursing rats' nests that only a terrier could dislodge – nay, not only living rats, but skeletons of rats that had lived, and gnawed, and decayed, years and years ago. We *may* come upon such a scandalous wreck of past management, and discover . . . an old enthusiast's collection of Chaucer autographs, deeds, customs' rolls, lost poems, what not? . . . now that searchers are so many.[42]

Archives were difficult to navigate and unpleasant to inhabit.

Decay was everywhere: small animals gnawed at the documents, which were fouled with dead bugs [sic] rodent excrement, worms, hairs, and nail clippings: old paper, vellum, and script were damaged by water, fumes, soot, extremes of temperature. Illegible writing, strange languages, shorthand, and secret codes all made archives places of mystery.[43]

They were also places of chaos, both disorganized and bothered. As early as 1873, Furnivall had sent out a plea to the Master of the Rolls, Sir T. Duffus Hardy (historian and archivist at the Record Office), stating that

every single original document drawn up or signed by Chaucer has disappeared from its proper place. Someone who knew the records thoroughly has systematically picked out – probably scores or hundreds of years ago – all Chaucer's work from every set of Records, and either stolen them or tied them up in some bundle which may be among the unindexed Miscellaneous Records. Through these records [I ask] for an official search, in the hope of recovering Chaucer's public receipts, accounts, &c.[44]

Such documents have never been found, and given the decay of the centuries and the haphazard methods of preservation, discovery seems unlikely.

Records were stored in a variety of locations, often unsafe. Some were housed in a temporary shed at the end of Westminster Hall and then moved to the King's Mews. Upon its destruction they were moved "to the stables of Caritou house, where 'Princess Charlotte used to take horse exercise.'"[45] The Domesday Book, accompanied by other records, was "kept in the Chapter House, behind which was a brewhouse and washhouse 'reported as dangerous,' of which Mr. Bulier made great fun in the House of Commons in 1835."[46] Every rescued and catalogued document was a cause célèbre.

Regardless of the chaos and clutter, scholars managed to work. Furnivall, as usual, bustled about soliciting subscriptions for his literary societies, hunting down translators and editors, conducting his own research, and denouncing scholarship he thought to be deficient. In 1874, for example, he shattered a theory on *The Parliament of Foules* published in the *Saturday Review*, because the author had not argued properly from the available public documents. The reviewer (unnamed) had declared that the "hero" of the poem was Enguerrand de Couci; the "heroine," Isabel Plantagenet; the date, February 14, 1364, "when Edward III entertained at Eltham King John of France." However, retorted Furnivall:

> This supposed theory I tested by documents at the Public Record Office. On February 14, Edward had been, not at Eltham, but at Westminster. The date on which he entertained King John was not February 14 but instead January 7 or 14.[47]

He concluded, "I only hope the *Saturday Review* will not continue this practice of publishing elaborate blunders about Chaucer."[48]

In 1882, Furnivall again appealed publicly to the Record Office as an aid against sloppy scholarship. This time he assaulted an unnamed "writer with much confidence" who had asserted that the park "walled with green stones" in Parliament was Woodstock, and that Chaucer knew Woodstock well. "Rubbish," cried Furnivall, who would admit to that assertion only if some "honest worker at the Public Record Office . . . will search the Patent Roll for the whole of the time that Chaucer was in service at court, and show us the day be day [sic] where the king was." He himself had undertaken such a search for 1363–1364 to prove that the author of a *Saturday Review* article had erred in his assumption. However, he continued,

> I haven't been able to find time for going on with these searches, or money to pay a Record-clerk to make them. But the work wants doing. Will any humble-minded admirer of the poet volunteer for it? If one will, I will print his results.[49]

Furnivall insisted on investigation and verification. On February 14, 1874, the *Manchester Times* noted that the Public Record Office had "just copied for Mr. Furnivall" Chaucer's accounts as Clerk of the Works for Westminster, the Tower of London, and the Castle of Berkhampstead, "which enrollment also contains a curious list of the dead stock ('mortui stauri') or utensils in the different palaces &c., received by Chaucer and given out by him, or handed over by him to his successor, John Gedney."[50] Furnivall once referred to himself proudly as a "scientific botanist."[51] To the fury of Swinburne (who considered *himself* to be an "aesthetic" critic), Furnivall trounced irresponsible methodology.

The founder of the Chaucer Society was clearly a powerful influence on Haweis's own scholarship, and the mention of his name throughout her work and her name throughout his reveals a supportive and affectionate relationship – quite apart from his friendship with the university-educated Spurgeon. Furnivall and Haweis corresponded with one another, worked together and shared library findings, and were scheduled for at least one common lecture series near the end of her life where *she* was to teach Chaucer and he the Old English epic. An article from *Lloyd's Weekly Newspaper* (Oct. 23, 1898, iss. 2918) announced the following:

Free Lectures for the People on "Glimpses of English Literature"

The first lecture will be given next Tuesday by Dr. F. J. Furnivall, when Dr. Macnamara will preside: on November 3, Mrs. Haweis will lecture on "The Canterbury Pilgrims."

But Mrs. Haweis died of a prolonged illness "toward the end of November" that same year. There is no proof that the lecture was ever delivered, at least, not by her.

Furnivall's knowledge of Haweis's Chaucer work was intimate. After her death, Hugh Reginald wrote to him:

> I do not know if it is asking too much of you to write down any appreciation you may have framed of my beloved wife especially as a born antiquarian and a student of Chaucer and any estimate of her Chaucer and antiquarian studies [sic] of course any amenities or episodes you can recall I shall be duly grateful.[52]

The Rev. Haweis did not go on to publish any projected memoirs and there is no extant record as to whether or not Furnivall ever granted his request. But as the following chapters will demonstrate, Furnivall and Mary Eliza shared a common philosophy on the study and dissemination of Chaucer materials, which would ultimately work to the detriment of Furnivall and to the downfall of Haweis. The two argued strongly against the idea that "either scholarship or criticism should be the exclusive preserve of the leisured class or indeed, the professional academic or librarian."[53]

> Chaucer studies after Furnivall were quickly assimilated into the academic study of English literature, and while Chaucer continues to be part of the mainstream of literary, poetic, and popular tradition, the published discourse of his works is increasingly contained within the tertiary education sector: the world of the professional Chaucerian.[54]

While Trigg notes that "Furnivall's version of medieval studies . . . had a popular and radical edge that had been missing in many academic programs in the twentieth century,"[55] she also quotes a letter from Walter Skeat to James Murray where Murray notes that "somehow [Furnivall] isn't believed at the universities . . . it has arisen from his off prefaces, etc., & modes of expression."[56] The same could be said of Haweis. His story is not complete without hers.

Furnivall's colleague Walter Rye (1843–1929), an athlete and genealogist, appears regularly in Haweis's scholarly notes. Rye would go on to write *Chaucer,*

A Norfolk Man (1915) and contribute to the *Life Records of Chaucer* (1900). Haweis knew him as a meticulous researcher, and there can be little doubt that his technique of searching for documents influenced hers. His book *Records and Record Searching*, published in 1888, gives testimony to his prodigious reading and acute sense of the chase. It provides a scholarly methodology for searching out materials to compile a pedigree, the history of a parish, a transfer of land. Rye lists and annotates scores of books one should consult; enumerates materials often housed in a "private Castle or old Mansion house"; catalogs specifics to be noted from architectural descriptions. He knew where reference sources were to be found, where partial reproductions had been printed, and where one might view a "recent photo-zincographic edition" of whatever one might be looking for.[57] He discusses the nature of the various rolls series, such as the Pipe and the Fine (where much of the Chaucer research was taking place) and he refers the reader to the *Gentleman's Magazine* or to specific volumes of *Notes & Queries* where additional articles on this and that had been written. Rye knew of materials not readily available to the average researcher, and he deplored the documents that could have been "transcribed for the press by unskilled labor" if it were generally known that they existed.[58] He knew exactly what had been calendared and what had not, and he recommended alternative manuscripts in case what one was searching for did not exist. *Records and Record Searching* is a thorough book on research methods that would satisfy even the strictest twenty-first-century scholars. Such a repository of sources was Rye that conducting archival research without consulting him must have been difficult. He had an amazing grasp both of the big picture and the minute detail. Haweis worked closely with him during her research on Chaucer. He crops up in *Chaucer for Children* and especially in *Chaucer for Schools* in connection with the location and physical state of documents.

It was in the British Library that Mary Eliza met Emanuel Deutsch, a brilliant Semitic scholar and orientalist who was twenty years her senior. A witty and distinguished conversationalist, he served as an assistant librarian under less than ideal conditions. Deutsch (who had taught Hebrew to George Eliot) had written *An Essay on the Talmud*, for which he had received critical acclaim. He and the Rev. Haweis were acquainted, and he and Mary Eliza developed a deep friendship – probably love on his part, if one can trust her diary – lasting until his death from stomach cancer in 1873. On May 29, 1871, she writes,

> In January (13th) Mr. Deutsch came to stay with us for a week or so, as he was very ill, & very uncomfortable in the lodgings he had: and the time has lengthened almost imperceptibly [into?] 5 months, for here he is still, and no better. He is a queer creature, better than the average man – I used to dislike him once, and think him plebian and ugly, and a bore: and now I am very fond of him, and respect him very much.

Haweis would lament her own youth and lack of wisdom during her time with Deutsch; she had only just begun writing fashion articles and nothing more substantive. She listened to him talk about Moorish literature and its influence on the West, particularly stories of tragic and unrequited love that filtered into her various Chaucer readings. Deutsch felt strongly that Arabic poetry could not be translated, that the changing of a single word could destroy the meaning. Haweis echoed this theory in her Chaucer texts when she argues for reading the poet in the original. Deutsch explained to her the principles of "electrobiology" and, apparently, its application to the magic tricks in *The Franklin's Tale*. In a later footnote in *Chaucer for Children*, she would pay tribute to him:

> It is quite clear that many of the tricks [of the jougleurs] were due to electro-biology [animal magnetism], a science known to those mighty cultivators and preservers of learning, the Arabs.

One might wish that she had elaborated on this idea, but instead, she refers Chaucer readers to the "Literary Remains of Emanuel Deutsch" with its two articles on Arabic poetry ("Early Arabic Poetry," "Arabic Poetry in Spain and Sicily") for a discussion of "what we owe to the Arabs, and of their influence upon mediaeval European literature."[59]

More familiar to contemporary Chaucerians than Emanuel Deutsch is Walford D. Selby (1845–1889), whose own work on the Chaucer seal would result in Haweis's most scholarly article. Selby was superintendent of the search room at the Record Office and founder of the Pipe Roll Society. He contributed articles on literary subjects for such periodicals as the *Athenæum* and the *Antiquary* and wrote "The Robbery of Chaucer at Hatcham" and "Chaucer as Forrester of Petherton in the County of Somerset" for the *Life-Records of Chaucer*.[60] In 1877, Selby published an article in the *Academy* concerning "two deeds of considerable curiosity, more especially to those interested in all that concerns the life and family history of 'the Father of English poetry.'"[61] These small parchment bundles contained a badly damaged seal bearing the legend, "S Ghofrai Chaucer,"[62] the coat not generally assigned to Chaucer: "Party per pale, argent and gules a bend counterchanged." This new seal showed "ermine on a chief three birds heads issuant." Because of the small size of the seal and the preponderance of birds used as heraldic devices, it was "difficult to determine the species of birds" pictured.

Haweis's reaction to this finding is noteworthy. In 1850, twenty-seven years before Selby's article, in the "unsorted masses of Her Majesty's Exchequer,"[63] Joseph Hunter, Fellow in the Society of Antiquaries, had come across a copy of a deed belonging to Thomas Chaucer, on which the seal of Geoffrey Chaucer had been affixed, and he wrote to Sir Henry Ellis, Secretary of the Society, describing his findings. Hunter sketched the seal, distinguished its armorial bearings, and invited the members of the society to view it. He observed that the "impression is in a good state of preservation. The inscription was not originally cut with much care, and one or two of the earlier letters are imperfect in the stamp; but it may be read thus: S' Ghofrai chaucier."[64]

In 1882, the year when the second edition of *Chaucer for Children* was published, Haweis also published the scholarly article for *Belgravia*, "More News of Geoffrey Chaucer." The material in this article supplements the notes to her revised children's book so exactly that one can know precisely how and where she researched the Chaucer seal and can gain extraordinary insight into the way she worked. Excited by Hunter's article and Selby's revival of it, she, too, visited the "miscellanea of the Queen's Remembrancer of the Exchequer,"[65] and she, too, sketched the seal in question and the seal of John Chaucer as well. Other critics, she noted, had debated the letter "G," thinking it might actually be a "T" for "Thomas." But, using her artist's power of observation, Haweis adds, "On close examination I cannot see how the unmistakable "F" can belong to the word Thomas, and it seems to me all but proved to be Geoffrey's seal." Hunter had described a pelican on the reverse side of the seal, but Haweis is not so certain: it is not "clear," she remarks; it may be a "heron," consistent with John Chaucer's mother's previous name, "Heroun." But while Hunter had been content with a mere superficial rendering of the seal, Haweis was not. Her curiosity over the seal and over Thomas Chaucer's failure to take the Chaucer arms led her back to the manuscript evidence.

Like the document from the Exchequer, the Cottonian, MS. Julius C. VII. F. 153 also contains a drawing of Thomas Chaucer's seal, with the accepted coat and crest. On the crest of the latter is a unicorn's head, but "in the corner of the seal is a *bird* [sic]." Haweis notes:

> Although [Thomas] relinquished the arms of Chaucer for those of Roet . . . the retention of the bird on his seal (Cotton, MS.) corresponds curiously with the birds' heads upon John Chaucer's seal, and may be the paternal emblem, which the vintner's grandson still bore.[66]

The *presence* of the bird is more important than the *species*, she notes: "The fourth generation may have remembered a bird, but forgotten *what* bird, or why it was there."[67] Regardless, "a seal and arms were only used by persons of good position"; Haweis's assumption is that both Thomas Chaucer and his father were persons of class.

This incident with the seal not only reveals Haweis's acute intellectual inquisitiveness, it also gives additional insight into her relationship with Furnivall, who could not resist taunting her about her discovery. In the *Academy* of July 22, 1882, he wrote the following "tit-bit":

Chaucer and the Herons

The first question is Are [sic] the things on John Chaucer's seal heron heads at all? Judging from Mrs. Haweis's drawing of them, I can only say that things less like heron's heads I have seldom seen. Unable to make out what they were, I turned the seal upside down, and then saw that the supposed heron's heads were – or looked extremely – like three pairs of half-boots, meant I suppose for *chausses*. The term was used for shoes as well as hose, and would, I think, include anything that the Chaucer – the hose- or shoe-maker – might manufacture. At present, I don't believe in the "herons" one bit, though I can't assert that the half-boots upside down may not be meant for birds' heads.

F. J. Furnivall

PS. My friend Mr. Walford D. Selby, of the Public Record Office, has again carefully examined John Chaucer's seal and says that the things questioned "are birds' heads undoubtedly." His judgment is final. I can then only say that the heads are far too stumpy for long-billed herons' heads.

In a note in the *Athenæum* written on October 5, 1901, J. Hamilton Wylie, commenting on the relationship between Thomas Chaucer and Geoffrey, either did not know of Haweis's assertion or ignored it. He writes:

The seal attached to this [Public Record Office] document is certainly the seal of Thomas Chaucer; and on it can be made out a portion of the bird (possibly a *swan* [emphasis mine]) which appears on the seal of Geoffrey Chaucer.

In addition to Selby, Furnivall, Rye, and Deutsch, Mary Eliza worked alongside historian John Richard Green, who had served as best man at the Haweis wedding and who is now considered one of the earliest social historians.

Green was the first to regard social history as of comparable importance to political, constitutional history. . . . the elements of social, intellectual and urban history, with which he broke new ground by introducing into his narrative, have now become accepted currency.[68]

Haweis wove elements of social, intellectual, and urban history into her text as well. Her diary reveals a close relationship between herself and Green. Green published his *Short History of the English People* in 1874, at the same time that Haweis was working on *Chaucer for Children*. The two works reveal a startling influence on one another.

Excerpts from Haweis's diary demonstrate this alliance clearly. In the preface to *A Short History*, Green states that he is not concerned with "details of foreign wars and diplomacies, the personal adventures of kings and nobles, the pomp of courts, or the intrigues of favourites" but with people themselves, and therefore "I have devoted more space to *Chaucer than to Cressy*" (emphasis mine).[69] This shift in emphasis can be traced directly to Haweis. In the archives at the University of British Columbia is a draft of a speech designed for an "at home" lecture in 1890. On page 3, Haweis read the following, which she had recycled, and although lengthy it merits quoting in full:

I remember Mr J. R. Green, the historian, a man full of insight & grasp, saying to me when I first began to love Chaucer, though he praised my enterprise – "Of course Chaucer's worst fault is his dullness. All his manes will fit any characters, & he wastes time describing their millinery." I was but a beginner, but I could not brook that. I said "There is *no* modern novelist whose characters are as differentiated, so clearly contrasted. What you call the "millinery" is the description of the outer man as interpreting the inner man, which was necessary in an age of sumptuary laws, & when dress was held (at least in Florence) as a proper external expression of character or vocation. Chaucer is a great romanticist, & an artist to the finger tip.

Mr Green who was a very kind & indulgent friend to me, remained silent. He had not then read Chaucer with any attention. Later whilst writing his "Short History", he came to me and said,

> "You are quite right. There is an enormous amount in Chaucer which I never noticed before. Indeed I should imagine there was hardly a subject on earth which Chaucer does not *effleurer*. One might learn from him the condition of knowledge, & thought, & religion, manners & the arts, medicine & all the sciences in England in the 14th cent:" So said J.R. Green. I then had the sweet satisfaction of replying "I told you so; and the more you read him the more depth in him you will discover." Mr Green also once said to me that there was a painful absence in Chaucer of the love of children, or allusions to them. Mr. Green was singularly devoted to children. I was able to show him half a dozen extremely sympathetic passages concerning children of all ages. These are just instances of the misapprehensions that Chaucer [?] even by cultivated minds. I am glad to remember my Chaucer talks with Mr. Green, who was certainly a convert worth making.[70]

Haweis would repeat this story many times during her academic life. Green's conversion is reflected in his *Short History* by his extended description of Chaucer as a "universal" poet, a creator of "distinct figures." He writes:

> It is the first time in English poetry that we are brought face to face not with characters or allegories or reminiscences of the past with living and breathing men, men distinct in temper and sentiment as in face and costume or mode of speech.[71]

In her Chaucer sessions with Green, Haweis had taught him well. More space is devoted to Chaucer than to the Danish kings or to the Black Death.

Yet Haweis's influence on Green was cosmetic only. As Bellamy, Laurence, and Perry observe, "in many cases the endeavors [by nineteenth-century women] to give their own work authority amounted to providing intellectual sustenance for men working in the same field."[72] Green was openly scornful of antiquarian pursuits, "candidly and cheerfully admit[ting] his own ignorance of archives and documents":

> I didn't dare tell him [Joseph Burtt – an Assistant Keeper at the Public Record Office] . . . the worst of the matter, namely that I had never seen a "Roll" or

read a manuscript in my life. Of course, bore as it is, one must "work at the Rolls," but it seems to me that the Burtt and Hartshorne school forget that these may supplement and correct history, but they can never *be* history.[73]

Ironically, and in her own way, Haweis was the better "historian" of the two.

This is perhaps the first time one can actually document Haweis's literary influence behind the scenes. Green's book "met with a success unprecedented since the days of Maccaulay."[74] It was a work of "extraordinary popularity" that influenced scores of readers who might not have turned to Haweis's works. But those are *her* ideas Green perpetuates, and not originally his own. Although he cannot resist noting that "in some of the stories . . . composed no doubt at an earlier time, there is the tedium of the old romance or of the pedantry of the schoolman,"[75] he is unequivocally converted.

However, we do know that Green *did* read *Chaucer for Children* in the proof stage and offered suggestions for improvement. Ironically, he wanted more of Chaucer as a *poet* than Chaucer as an historical figure, and he hoped that Haweis would

> soon be writing about Chaucer for older folk. There were bits of criticism that are so full of insight and at the same time also contain a [temperateness?] that they quite warrant for setting out on a longer journey. As it is, I think you have hit the child-level admirably without sinking into childhood drivel of a mawkish sort.[76]

Green ends his letter with the words, "You are not a woman of genius," and there is no clue to his tone. At the end he had glued a clipping from the newspaper about her book that took an ambivalent stand.[77]

There is no evidence that Green ever publicly promoted Mary Eliza's work, although there is some indication that he might have neglected her purposefully. In 1877, the same year as the publication of *Chaucer for Children*, Green wrote a letter to Furnivall, proposing a 140-page "Chaucer primer" for "would-be-intelligent-readers-of Chaucer." He outlined five chapters: (1) English literature before Chaucer; (2) the poet's life in pictures; (3) an account of the poems in chronological order; (4) Chaucer's influence; and (5) a Chaucer bibliography. Even though *Chaucer for Children* had been a success and Haweis was no doubt planning her *Chaucer for Schools*, Green apparently did not ask her to write his proposed text. Instead, he asked Furnivall to do it himself, but Furnivall turned it down. In 1893, the work was published as *Chaucer's Canterbury Tales*, authored by Alfred W. Pollard. Its reviews were less than stellar:

> This edition is a good one for those whom the editor apparently had in mind: persons of literary taste who want to know something about Chaucer without bothering to find out just what he said or how he said it.[78]

Richard Green and Mary Eliza seem to have had a volatile relationship. A clue to Green's apparent affront may be found in Haweis's diary, whose pages are filled with regular references to Green that are not always favorable. She accused him of being "as spiteful as a women" and "jealous of Deutsch." She also remarked on July 26 (n.d.): "I won't go to any more picture galleries with him at present."

Still, Haweis may have owed to him *Chaucer for Schools'* "Table of Historical Events" similar to his "Chronological Annuals of English History," since she is the only contemporary Chaucer editor to include one. And she continued to influence him. In 1878, four years after Green's history appeared, Boston's *Literary World* published a long article on Chaucer. It contains Haweis's (unattributed) ideas direct from *The Short History of the English People.*[79]

While Haweis's discoveries often go often unheralded, one such finding apparently did not: that of the dubious parentage of Thomas Chaucer. In the *Belgravia* article, Haweis included a section on "Chaucer's Children," where she refers to a letter written in 1402 to Henry IV by his son, Prince Harry.[80] In the letter, the prince points to Thomas Chaucer as his "cousin." Haweis continues that even though this term was often used to refer to individuals not blood-related, such persons were usually of noble birth; Thomas Chaucer was not. If the term were used literally, it implies a closer connection between Thomas Chaucer and John of Gaunt than previously supposed. At this point, Haweis's prose, which is generally clear, seems purposefully ambiguous:

> [The letter] confirms the Roet-Chaucer alliance, inasmuch as John of Gaunt's children by Katherine would have been actually first cousins to Philippa Roet's children: and John's son by Blanche of Lancaster was therefore a sort of connection: rendering it reasonable, though by great indulgence, for Thomas Chaucer, if of Roet descent, to claim actual cousinship with John of Gaunt's son's son, whom he may have been guardian to according to the above letter.[81]

If Thomas was incontestably Geoffrey's son, she asks, why did he not erect a rich monument on his father's grave, as he had done on his own wife Alice's?[82] Why did Chaucer never speak of his first son, as he spoke of "little Lewis"?

Haweis paints a bold scenario, one that is familiar in its general outline to modern-day Chaucer scholars. She presupposes that Thomas was born about 1372–1374, when Chaucer was almost consistently away from England. During that time, Philippa, like other maids of honor, would have been a resident in the Savoy Palace, in proximity to the duke. Gaunt made handsome provisions for Philippa and Thomas from the time of Thomas's birth. There were also grants to Chaucer himself, but they were less generous and diminished after Philippa's death. When the poet was in dire poverty during the end of Richard II's reign, Thomas apparently "neglected" him. (As proof of Chaucer's "pecuniary difficulties," Haweis cites a record in which Isabella Bukholt sued the poet for debt. The sheriff's response was "*nichil habet*"!)[83] Haweis notes "Chaucer's ceaseless hits at untrusty [sic] wives" throughout his poetry and the lawsuit with Cecilia Champaigne, where Haweis stops just short of implying payback. Thomas's surrender of the poet's arms in favor of those of his mother seem almost a natural consequence of this story line, as does Prince Harry's peculiar use of the word "cousin" cited earlier.

Haweis ends this section as equivocally as she began it. The medieval court was not a place where morals were taught: "few [individuals] were strict." "Not that Chaucer himself was worse than the common run of courtiers . . . nor that his wife was worse than her sister, or as bad."[84] Surrounded by some of the "fairest and highest bred women in England, Chaucer may have felt it impolite to quarrel with his bread-and-butter, even if it had now and then a bitter taste." Chaucer was "canny" and might have opted for a post that kept him closer to home.[85]

Was Mary Eliza Haweis the first to advance the Thomas Chaucer/John of Gaunt theory? Contemporaries apparently thought so. By 1892 the theory was so controversial and well known that it did not have to be explained. An anonymous reviewer of Lounsbury's *Studies in Chaucer*, for example, commended Lounsbury for asserting that the weight of parental evidence was in favor of Thomas being the poet's son. "And to this all sober reasoners [sic] will subscribe. The disagreeable guess elaborated by Mrs. Haweis is not even alluded to."[86] The reviewer was George Lyman Kittredge, who seems either not to have read Lounsbury's book or to have read it in haste. Lounsbury (an American academic) actually devoted seven pages to the hypothesis, which he nowhere describes as offensive. He gives Haweis credit (in his notes) not only for bringing the theory of Thomas's dubious parentage before the public, but also for discovering the letter written to King Henry IV containing the problematic word "cousin." Lounsbury himself remains uncommitted. Believing that further discoveries might resolve the issue, he concludes:

> It is perhaps unsafe to say more than this, that in the light of our present knowledge kinship of some kind must have existed between Geoffrey Chaucer and Thomas Chaucer. This may or may not have been that of father and son, but the weight of evidence at present is strongly in favor of that particular relationship.[87]

In 1932, Russell Krauss published *Three Chaucer Studies: I. Chaucerian Problems: Especially the Petherton Forestership and the Question of Thomas Chaucer*, which argued in favor of the illegitimacy. In his review of Krauss, B. J. Whiting noted that

> [Krauss's] investigations have forced him, somewhat against his own will, to the conclusion that Thomas Chaucer was the illegitimate son of John of Gaunt, conceived several years after Philippa's marriage to Geoffrey. This opinion was advanced as early as 1882 by Mrs. Haweis and echoed, without acknowledgment, by Edward Walford in 1888. J. W. Hales attacked Walford's statement, set forth with curious and undocumented confidence. Mr. Krauss suggests that it was Hales['] Victorianism which moved him to reject this tempting assumption, and feels that we of a new and modern era need to be less squeamish.[88]

Whiting is intrigued by the theory and wonders if Chaucer "read of naughty wives to an audience which knew his wife to be delinquent, perhaps in the very presence of that wife and her paramour."[89] He concludes, however, that such a shame would have been "as abhorrent to Chaucer's generation as to our own."[90] He returns to the argument: "It is almost incredible that John [of Gaunt's] parenthood, had it existed, should not have been known or guessed at, and recorded, between the event and Mrs. Haweis."[91] Not entirely convinced that the problem is solved, Whiting nevertheless dismisses the theory as untrue.

Haweis's name was still connected with Thomas's paternity theory when John Manly wrote his review of Krauss's book.[92] Manly adds Krauss to such proponents as Haweis, L. B. Walford, and Walter Rye, and condemns them all for shoddy research and for rushing to publish. But soon thereafter, Haweis's name vanishes from the group. She is missing from both Root's and Young's review of *Thomas Chaucer*.[93] She never figures in John Gardner's lengthy summary of the problem in *The Life and Times of Chaucer*, nor in Robinson's edition; Howard's *Chaucer: His Life, His Works, His World*; or the *Riverside*. In 1992, when Derek Pearsall wrote *The Life of Geoffrey Chaucer*, the theory is restricted to a clause and a note. Pearsall refers the reader to Martin B. Ruud's 1926 *Thomas Chaucer* and to Russell Krauss.[94]

Notes

1 F. J. Furnivall, "Recent Work on Chaucer," *Macmillan's Magazine* 27 (1873): 383–393.
2 Ibid., 390–393.
3 John W. Hales, *Notes and Essays on Shakespeare* (London: G. Bell & Sons, 1884). Hales notes that while the influence of Chaucer is most apparent in *The Knight's Tale* and *Troylus and Cryseyde*, his input can be found in *A Midsummer's Night's Dream*, *Two Noble Kinsmen*, *Venus and Adonis*, *Tarquin and Lucrece*, and *Romeo and Juliet* as well. It is also in the *Tale of Gamelyn* (that Shakespeare erroneously thought Chaucer wrote). Besides these obvious connections, "there are scattered throughout Shakespeare's plays and poems various other indications that the writings of Chaucer were anything but a sealed or an unopened book to him" (ibid., 90–91).
4 William Minto, *Characteristics of English Poets from Chaucer to Shirley* (Edinburgh: Blackwood & Sons, 1874). Minto's biography is a generalized sweep of the text of *The Canterbury Tales*, relying on plot synopsis and various Chaucer phrases for adulation.
5 *Trewman's Exeter Flying Post*, 27 Jan. 1875: iss. 5746.
6 Walford D. Selby, *The Life Records of Chaucer* (London: Kegan Paul, Trench, Trübner, 1875), 57, 59. Published for the Chaucer Society.
7 Mark W. Turner, "Time, Periodicals, and Literary Studies," *Victorian Periodicals Review* 39:4 (Winter 2006): 209.
8 Kate Sanborn, "One View of Chaucer Mania," *Manhattan* 3 (1883): 307. Mark W. Turner discusses the need for a systematic study of Victorian periodicals and the near impossibility of using them for comprehensive research. Turner, "Time, Periodicals, and Literary Studies."
9 *Glasgow Herald*, 20 June 1872: iss. 1002. For recent studies on Chaucer's tomb see Joseph A. Dane, *Who Is Buried in Chaucer's Tomb?* (East Lansing: Michigan State University Press, 1988). See also Dane and Alexandra Gillespie, "Back at Chaucer's Tomb: Chaucer's 'Workes'," *Studies in Bibliography* 52 (1999): 89–96; Thomas A. Pendergast, *Chaucer's Dead Body* (New York: Routledge, 2004).
10 *Birmingham Daily Post*, 14 Dec. 1868: iss. 1002.

11 Ibid.
12 See, for example, *Reynold's Newspaper*, 10 July 1853; *Lloyd's Weekly Newspaper*, 20 Dec. 1863; *Birmingham Daily Post*, 28 Dec. 1874.
13 *Penny Illustrated Paper*, 26 Dec. 1863: p. 422.
14 *Graphic*, 15 Nov. 1873: iss. 8598.
15 *Manchester Times*, 23 Sept. 1876.
16 *Derby Mercury*, 28 Apr. 1875.
17 P. Lindner, "Alliteration in Chaucer," *Academy* 7 (1865): 554.
18 UBC, MEH Box 1, Misc. Box 31, n.d. Haweis's title for this document is not clear. It may be "News."
19 Unattributed magazine article, "Adviser to the Victorians," MEH 2A Biographical folder #3, Box 31, UBC.
20 Colin Cunningham, "Hints on Household Taste and the Art of Decoration: Authors, Their Audiences and Gender in Interior Design," in *Women Scholarship and Criticism*, eds. Joan Bellamy, Anne Laurence, and Gillian Perry (Manchester: Manchester University Press, 2001), 159–187.
21 UBC, MEH Box 1, Misc. Box 31, n.d.
22 Ibid.
23 H.R. Haweis, "Words for Women," quoted by Bea Howe, in *Arbiter of Elegance* (London: Harvill Press, 1967), 149.
24 Mark Taylor, "Coloured Houses: Transgressing the Limits of the Domestic Realm," in *Limits: Proceedings from the 21st Annual Conference of the Society of Architectural Historians*, eds. Harriet Edquest and Hélène Frichot (Australia & New Zealand: RMIT University), 461–466.
25 UBC, MEH 2A Biographical folder # 3, Box 31. Anonymous article. n.d. The subtitle of this article reads: "The story of Mrs. Haweis who, in the 'Nineties' became as much a household figure as Mrs. Beeton, and whose advice on 'Fashion and on the Home' makes good sense to-day." Mary Isabella Beeton (1836–1865) wrote a book on middle-class household management, popular during the Victorian era. *The Mirror of Literature* contained historical narratives, biographical memoirs, manners and customs, topographical descriptions, discoveries in the arts and sciences, and, coincidentally, quite a few articles on Chaucer. A copy of this journal can be found at http://books.google.com/books?id=lbwRAAAAYAAJ&printsec=titlepage&vq=chaucer&source=gbs_v2_summary_r&cad=0.
26 MEH Box 1, Misc, Box 31. "Sprat," in this case, seems to be used ironically, as a term of contempt (*Oxford English Dictionary*, s.v.).
27 What follows is drawn from Haweis, UBC, Box 22, folder 4–6. There are no page numbers on this material and only an occasional date.
28 F.W. Maitland, *Athenæum*, 8 Dec. 1906. For a summary of Bateson's medieval career, see Mary Dockray Miller, "Mary Bateson (1865–1906): Scholar and Suffragist," in *Women Medievalists and the Academy*, ed. Jane Chance (Madison: University of Wisconsin Press, 2004), 67–78, 76.
29 Miller, *Women Medievalists and the Academy*, 72.
30 Renate Haas, "Caroline F.E. Spurgeon (1869–1942): The First Woman Professor in England," in *Women Medievalists and the Academy*, ed. Jane Chance (Madison: University of Wisconsin Press, 2004), 102–103.
31 G.B. Burgin, "Some British Museum Stories: A Chat with Dr. Garnett," *Ideler* 5 (July 1894): 374. Burgin remembers "one lady who came to see a cookery book with a particular plate prefixed illustrating a certain method of carving. She was warned in a dream that if she came to the Reading Room of the British Museum, she would find it. She came, spoke to me, and, curiously enough, I remembered a cookery book which had belonged to my father, and sent for it, and there was the identical plate. She copied it and went away rejoicing" (ibid.).

32 My thanks to Miss Georgina Chetwynd, Archives Assistant at the British Museum, for supplying me with this information (personal email 14 October 2004).

33 The exhibit of the Lewis Chessmen was orchestrated by Sir Frederick Madden. http://www.metmuseum.org/about-the-museum/press-room/exhibitions/2011/the-game-of-kings-medieval-ivory-chessmen-from-the-isle-of-lewis.

34 Philippa Levine, *The Amateur and the Professional* (London: Cambridge University Press, 1986), 36. For a discussion of twentieth-century *scientists* conducting such "seminars" with technological assistance, see David Crane, "A Test of the Invisible College," *American Sociological Review* (1969): 335–352.

35 Levine, *The Amateur and the Professional*, 87.

36 Bonnie G. Smith, *The Gender of History* (Cambridge: Cambridge University Press, 1996), 107.

37 Levine, *The Amateur and the Professional*, 37.

38 Ibid., 87.

39 Mary Eliza Haweis, "More News of Chaucer," *Belgravia* 48 (1882): Pt. I, 40–41.

40 "Annual Reports of the Deputy Keeper of the Public Records," *London Quarterly Review* 26:51 (1886): 57.

41 Ibid.

42 Haweis, "More News of Chaucer," 45–46.

43 Bonnie G. Smith, *The Gender of History* (Cambridge, 1995), 119.

44 *Leicester Chronicle*, 27 June 1835.

45 *Newcastle Courant*, 12 Dec. 1873.

46 *Pall Mall Gazette*, 15 Jan. 1896: iss. 9612.

47 F. W. Furnivall, "The Saturday Review on Chaucer's *Canterbury Tales*," *Academy*, Feb. 1874: 174.

48 Ibid.

49 *Academy*, no. 519, 15 Apr. 1882: 269.

50 *Saturday Review*, 14 Feb. 1874.

51 Robert Sawyer, "Furnivall and the Scientific Method," http://borrowers.uga.edu/cicoon/borrowers/request?id=781463.

52 Response from King's College London, Furnivall archives via my request for any papers from the Rev. Haweis, n.d.

53 Suzy Anger, *Victorian Interpretations* (Ithaca, NY: Cornell University Press, 2005), 134.

54 Stephanie Trigg, *Congenial Souls* (Minneapolis: University of Minnesota Press, 2002), 185.

55 Ibid., 188.

56 William Benzie, *Dr. F. J. Furnivall: Victorian Scholar Adventurer* (Norman, OK: Pilgrim Books, 1983), 105.

57 Walter Rye, *Records and Record Searching* (London: E. Stock, 1888), 25n5.

58 Ibid., 5.

59 Mary Eliza Haweis, *Chaucer for Children* (London: Chatto & Windus, 1877), p. 86.

60 Selby, *The Life Records of Chaucer*, 57–58.

61 *Academy*, 18 Oct. 1877: 364.

62 Ibid.

63 *Morning Chronicle*, 31 May 1850: 20652; *Glasgow Herald*, 13 Nov. 1886: 272.

64 Joseph Hunter, "The Seal of Chaucer: Copy of the Deed to Which Is Appended: Copy of Public Instrument Notifying to Him His Removal from His Office of Clerk of the King's Works," *Archaeologia* 34 (1852): 42–45.

65 Haweis, "More News of Chaucer," 40.

66 Ibid., 40–41.

67 Ibid., 40.

68 Roger Hudson, Introduction to, *A Short History of the English People*, by John Richard Green (1874; reprint, London: Folio Society, 1992), xiii.

69 Green, *A Short History of the English People*, xxiii.

70 UBC Box 29–7, "Lecture Notes."
71 Green, *A Short History of the English People*, 223.
72 Joan Bellamy, Anne Laurence, and Gillian Perry, eds., *Women, Scholarship and Criticism: Gender and Knowledge, c. 1790–1900* (Manchester: Manchester University Press, 2000), 13.
73 As quoted in Levine, *The Amateur and the Professional*, 30. Rev. C.H. Hartshorne had published *The Book of Rarities in the University of Cambridge, Illustrated by Original Letters and Notes, Biographical, Literary, and Antiquarian* (London: Longman, 1829). Levine notes that with the popularity of archival research, men such as Freeman and Green (who refused to do it) had . . . been ousted at the end of the century, by meticulous scholars such as Maitland, Gardiner, and others.
74 http://www.bartelby.org/224/0217.html. In 1878, George Barnett Smith, reviewer for the *International Review* 5 (Mar. 1878) referred to Green's volume as "a work which has obtained so great a popularity that upwards of fifty thousand copies have been disposed of within a brief period. . . . No works of praise can be too great for the thoroughness of Mr. Green's treatment of his important subject" (n.p.).
75 Green, *A Short History of the English People*, 223.
76 Green's letter can be found under miscellaneous papers and "scraps" in the MEH, UBC archives. Another hand, possibly Mary Eliza's, but maybe her son Stephen's, has written at the top, "Letter from John Richard Green to Ms Haweis about proof of *Chaucer for Children*. There is no other form of identification.
77 Green, *A Short History of the English People*.
78 Rev. George Hempl, "Chaucer's Canterbury Tales," *MLN* 10:3 (Mar. 1895): 180.
79 June 1, 1878; 9:1.
80 Haweis, "More News of Chaucer," 43.
81 Ibid.
82 Ibid. Thomas's wife was Maud; his daughter, Alice.
83 Ibid., 44n1.
84 Haweis, "More News of Chaucer," 45.
85 Ibid.
86 George Lyman Kittredge, *Atlantic Monthly* 69 (Apr. 1892): iss. 414.
87 Lounsbury, "Studies in Chaucer," 112.
88 Rev. B.J. Whiting, *Three Chaucer Studies*, by Russell Krauss, Haldeen Braddy, and C. Robert Kase. *Speculum* 8:4 (1933): 532.
89 Ibid.
90 Ibid.
91 Ibid., 535.
92 John Manly, "Three Recent Chaucer Studies," *Review of English Studies* 10:30 (1934): 262.
93 Ibid.
94 See, respectively, *MLN* 42:1 (Jan. 1927): 56–58 and *Review of English Studies*, 3:9 (Jan. 1927): 80–93. See 318n4.

2 Chaucer's *Golden Key*

And surely those who know Chaucer, his roguish fun, his love of nature, birds, and books, his fresh boy's heart, his care to teach Lewys, his "lytel sone," must feel that there is in him very much to draw children to him, and will be glad at least to try whether Mrs. Haweis's pretty book – from the daisies on its cover to its "Notes on the Pictures" at the end, a labour of love – will not bring their little ones some of the sunshine and pleasure that the old poet has so often given to themselves.

Anonymous, *Academy*, 1876

It is a pleasant sign of the times that a book written for children by a lady should be constructed almost as carefully as if it had been written by a professor for his class.

Anonymous, *Saturday Review*, 1876

Chaucer for Children: A Golden Key appeared in time for the holidays. On December 23, 1876, the *Academy* proudly acclaimed that it must "take a high place among the Christmas and New Year's books of the season."[1] An attractive volume, bound and illustrated by Haweis herself, its cover displayed scenes from *The Canterbury Tales*, and inside it contained the *General Prologue*, five tales, and several of Chaucer's shorter lyrics. It was illustrated with eight colored pictures, twenty-eight woodcuts, and other incidental sketches; it also included a "Forewords to the Mother" [sic], and a long essay on "Chaucer the Tale-Teller," ostensibly addressed to a juvenile audience. On the dedication page, underneath a portrait of an ethereal blonde child, were the words,

Chiefly for the Use and Pleasure of
MY LITTLE LIONEL
for whom I felt the need of some book of this kind,
I have arranged and illustrated this
CHAUCER STORY-BOOK

Lionel was seven years old.

The book scored highly with Haweis's female audience. For the Victorians, motherhood was woman's highest achievement, and for certain of the reviewers of this text Mary Eliza Haweis had attained this goal. A critic from the *Academy* rhapsodized:

> This book is, we understand, the outcome of Mrs. Haweis's telling and teaching Chaucer's stories to her own boy of five [sic], and this has the test of practical experience in favour of the attempt it recommends, to make the bright old poet's *Tales* a nursery-book.[2]

Mrs. Haweis was hailed as "an accomplished and right-hearted lady,"[3] "telling the tales in her own mother's talk" and now asking other mothers "to try the same plan with their boys and girls."[4] According to the *Literary World*, by 1880 "several thousand copies were sold."[5]

Haweis's "pretty book" for children would, however, prove a conundrum. Its author was actually not particularly interested either in mothers or in children, so this production – less an outcome of her tale-telling to Lionel (which she did do) than of her conversations and shared scholarship with the male Chaucerians in her life – became her own special contribution to Chaucer studies. Original in depth and scope, *Chaucer for Children* occupies a unique place alongside the works of Bell, Morris, Tyrwhitt, Wright, and Skeat. It teems with learned footnotes, readings from manuscript variants, snippets of foreign languages, and remnants of scholarly debates. It demonstrates firsthand knowledge of Chaucer's previous editors and of their analysis of the texts. In writing this text, Haweis wrote the only book that was available to her as a nineteenth-century woman desirous of being a scholar but unwilling to be anonymous or to go under the pseudonym of a man. But contrary to the views of the *Academy* critic, the tales are not simply "in mother's talk." Haweis's work is a rich repository of materials on Chaucer activities during the last quarter of the nineteenth century, and it reveals – more than single articles, notices, or editions do – both her own understanding and that of the male scholars who ultimately shaped the tradition we know today.

David Matthews, in *The Making of Middle English, 1765–1910,* refers to the larger history of individual manuscripts as "microhistories" and contends that scholars have ignored what is said in nineteenth-century Middle English editions. Twentieth- and twenty-first-century editors, who frequently lack the skill of individuals like Frederick Madden, often ignore earlier editors entirely:

> Middle English studies can be very forgetful indeed. Modern editions of *Piers Plowman* often make no reference to the sixteenth-century editions of the B-text. A recent and authoritative edition of *Confessio Amantis* does not record the dates of the early editions by Thomas Berthelette. It is true that there is a relative wealth of material on Chaucer scholarship through the centuries, but it is balanced by a great paucity in almost every other respect.[6]

Although earlier editions can be wildly speculative, Matthews notes that "something is lost when they are ignored." We fail to recognize that "prior authorities could once have been precisely as 'authoritative' as we now perceive modern authorities to be."[7]

Most contemporary reviewers were reticent to commend the efforts behind *Chaucer for Children*, finding its worthiness dubious. "Is Chaucer for children?" asked one critic:

> If not, and we can see nothing but a very distinct negative as answer to the question, is it quite right to present Chaucer to babes and sucklings as anything but what he is? We can but recall Spenser's scornful line [in describing the foolish philosopher who drew a crowd {*Faerie Queen*}], "And [he was] admired much by fools, women, and boys," with its terribly ingallant [sic] emphasis on the middle noun, and think what Chaucer himself would have said to the project of a nursery edition of the Pilgrimage."[8]

A reviewer for the *Daily News*, complaining about the "liberally provided" "original and philological notes" of the text, snorted in disbelief: "indeed every one of her closely-printed quarto pages bristles with explanations which seem to demand from the reader *a serious desire for knowledge*" (emphasis mine).[9] The writer continues:

> The climax of absurdity, however, seems to be reached in the compiler's list of "the principal authorities consulted," extending from Sir Samuel Meyrick's "Ancient Armour" to "Barbazan's Fabliaux and Contes, 1808"; though even this may be considered to be outdone by the maps of London in the 15th and in the 19th centuries, which the infant student is invited to study by the aid of numbered references. Even Mr. Skeat and Mr. Furnivall will probably agree that the zeal for a favorite study exhibited by the compiler of this book has a little outrun her discretion.[10]

Skeat and Furnivall, as it happened, did not agree, but Haweis's Chaucer book pitched about in murky waters.

Women who claimed to do scholarship on any level were not considered equal to men: "Critiques of their work normally referred to the author's gender, either praising her for manliness, or denigrating her for venturing into masculine territory where she was not fit to travel."[11] Amateurs were hit particularly hard, as their "history" was considered "worthless" and was lauded as such by male authors of professional journals.[12] Several years after the publication of Haweis's book, reviewers were still aggrieved. In 1878 a reviewer of Cowden Clarke's *Canterbury Chimes* remarked that "here [with Clarke's book] at last is a *real* 'Chaucer for Children' (emphasis mine) which all of young ages can read and enjoy without fear of phonetic spelling and lessons on punctuation hidden under pleasant tales."[13] From one extreme to another, however, both sets of critics had got it wrong. Like the iceberg, most of *Chaucer for Children* lay beneath the surface.

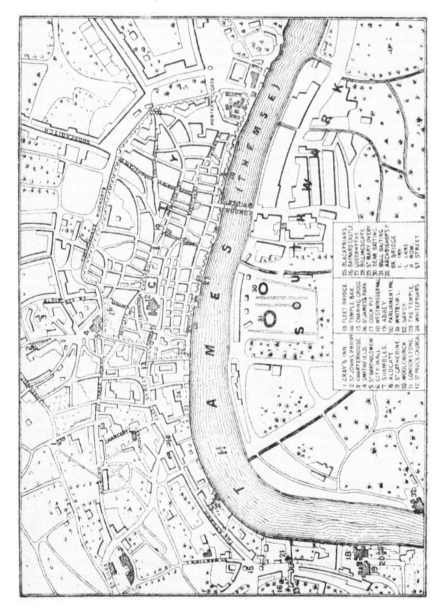

Figure 2.1 Fifteenth-century London map
Source: *Chaucer for Children.*

Among the brief notices and advertisements, the work of a single scholar stands apart. The anonymous author of the February 3, 1877, *Saturday Review* alone deemed Haweis worthy of serious study. This individual (undoubtedly a man, because women at the time did not read Chaucer this way) viewed her as unconventional and enterprising – qualities usually reserved for male authors. He wrote that, unlike Lamb in his *Tales from Shakespeare*, Mrs. Haweis

> comes with a bold and deliberate attempt to bring Chaucer himself, the difficult and remote – Chaucer himself, his very words and not his stories only – down to the comprehension of "my little Lionel." And it must be admitted that her attempt is both justifiable and in the main successful.[14]

Eschewing any domestic or sentimental qualities, he applauded her research, noting that she had sought out the best authorities, the best editions. Rather than confining her inside the walls of the nursery, he celebrated her scholarship, admiring her for keeping abreast of the latest discoveries of the Chaucer Society and for making the most of the few facts about the poet's life that remain ("since most of these are not personal documents but 'records of monies received by him'"). For this reader, Haweis is "a little too Lancastrian" and he occasionally wishes that she could argue from "stronger evidence." However, he concludes that by "endeavouring in all simplicity to follow her master without improving him [she] shows us how little is required to preserve the very essence of Chaucer."[15]

This is perhaps the first serious critique of a female scholar not connected, as Bateson and Spurgeon both would be, with the universities. Haweis was a woman who had never attended school and who had taught herself early on to read and write. What is the identity of this anonymous reviewer who had presumed to include Haweis among the elite male Chaucer group? His detailed knowledge of the Chaucer Society implies that he was a member himself. He is not Furnivall (he mentions Furnivall's contributions to Haweis's scholarship in an off-handed manner) and he is not Green (who did not know enough about Chaucer to write this way). Instead he was someone else who worked closely with her. He knew that other Chaucerians befriended her, and his comments on her bibliography – works by Barbazan and Le Grand, and "half a dozen editions of her poet" – indicate that he had read her work carefully. He noted that she had drawn on "Mr. Wright, and Sir S. Meyrick and Paul Lacroix" for her social history (no mention of Green here), and he remarked upon the effectiveness of her maps that contrast medieval and modern London during Chaucer's times. Carefully examining her woodcuts of the pilgrims, he compared the details appreciatively to those in Chaucer's texts.

This unknown individual is the audience that Haweis sought. Quickly leaving the mothers and children in her text behind, she turned her attention to academics and to word derivations from Middle English, French, Latin, and Arabic. She wrote about "crochets" and "quavers" in the music of Chaucer's lines and scanned long passages. She wrote one entire section on metrics, on the disyllable, and on the emphasis on the final -*e*, drawing the pronunciation from French and German.

In her treatment of philology, Haweis was strongly influenced by the works of Alexander J. Ellis (possibly the prototype for Professor Henry Higgins), whose work *Early English Pronunciation with Especial Reference to Shakespeare and Chaucer* appeared in 1869.[16] In the introduction to her *Chaucer for Children*, Haweis refers to him as "friend," and along with Furnivall thanks him for his "advice, assistance, and encouragement"(*CC*, p. xiv). She clearly admired his very technical scholarship, and her lucid paraphrase of the sections on the pronunciation of vowels, the treatment of the final -*e* at the ends of verbs, infinitives, medial elisions, and the metrical peculiarities of individual lines gives testimony to her knowledge and assimilation of these contemporary critical issues. Drawing analogies from German, French, and various Scottish dialects, she carefully forged relationships between rhythm and language sounds, urging the "home-schooling mother" to practice the correct pronunciation of Chaucer's opening reverdie, so that the child could hear the language. She adds,

> I think that anyone reading these lines over twice as I have roughly indicated will find the accent one not difficult to practice; and the perfect rhythm and ring of the line facilitates matters, as the ear can easily guide the pronunciation.
>
> (*CC*, pp. xv–xvi)

Ellis, after instructing his adult readers on sounding Chaucer's vowels and diphthongs (as a preparation for reading the *General Prologue*), remarks as follows:

> If the reader will bear these directions in mind and remember to pronounce with a general broad tone, rather Germanesque or provincial, he will have no difficulty in reading out the following prologue, and when he has attained facility in reading for himself, or has an opportunity of hearing others read in this way, he will be able to judge of the result, but not before.[17]

Haweis had appropriated this method.

The format of *Chaucer for Children* is in some ways similar to earlier scholarly editions of the poet's work. Preceding the dual-lingual text (Haweis, who despised modern editions of Chaucer, supplied her own translations) is an introduction to "Chaucer the Tale-Teller," a brief section on Chaucer's pilgrims and the *General Prologue*, and five of the tales: the *Knight's*, the *Friar's*, the *Clerk's*, the *Franklin's*, and the *Pardoner's*. She also included "Complaint of Chaucer to his Purse," "Two Rondeaux," "Virelai," and the "Good Counsel of Chaucer." Each poem is followed by a short interpretative essay by the author – actually the forerunner of the scholarly article entitled "Notes by the Way." The book ends with the section, "Notes on the Pictures" (pp. 107–112), an analysis of her colored plates and woodcuts and the manuscript sources that inspired her.

Pitching once again to mothers and children, Haweis asks:

> Do you like hearing stories? I am going to tell you of someone who lived a very long time ago, and who was a very wise and good man, and who told more wonderful stories than I shall be able to tell you in this little book.
>
> (*CC*, p. 1)

She continues, "Chaucer lived in England 500 years ago – a longer time than such a little boy as you can even think of." "How funny you would think he looked, if you could see him sitting in his house!" (*CC*, pp. 1–2). "I like to believe that [his wife] had long yellow hair, which Chaucer describes so often and so prettily" (*CC*, p. 5); or "If you could suddenly spring back into the time when Chaucer lived, what a funny world you would find!" (*CC*, p. 1). "When a lady walked out of doors, she had tall clogs to save her pretty shoes from the mud of the rough streets" (*CC*, p. 6). Chaucer wore "red stockings and black boots"; "he made fun of people in a merry way"; "his London was different from our London; and, oh, so much prettier." Then, in a manner almost wrenching, she deflects to the scholar, setting her base text and stating her rationale:

> I have adhered generally to [Richard] Morris's text (1866), as being both good and popular, only checking it by his Clarendon Press edition, and by Tyrwhitt, Skeat, and Bell, &c., when I conceived force is gained.
>
> (*CC*, p. xiv)

Children would be oblivious to Chaucer's previous editors, but scholars would not. Morris's Chaucer edition was the first to be based on manuscripts since that of Thomas Tyrwhitt, and his book had been popular (*Dictionary of National Biography*, s.v.). Morris had, in turn, influenced Skeat (who often copied him without citation).[18] Haweis's work is a palimpsest, revealing insights into her own manuscript research, new readings of Chaucer's text, and the once stormy, now obliterated, disputes of nineteenth-century scholars.

Haweis was secure in her own carefully accumulated knowledge and did not hesitate to disagree with established critics. She quarreled frequently with Robert Bell, who had published an eight-volume series of *Chaucer's Poetical Works* in 1884–1886, and also with Thomas Speght. Consider the "embrowdid" Squire from the *General Prologue* (l. 89), glossed simply by modern editors as "embroidered":

> Mr. Bell considers that these two lines ["Embrowdid was he, as it were a mede / Al full of fresshe floures, white and reede"] refer to the Squire's complexion of red and white. Speght thinks it means freckled. But there is little doubt that the material of his dress is what Chaucer means, for there is no other instance of Chaucer calling a complexion embroidered, and gorgeously flowered fabrics embroidered with the needle were peculiar to the period and in common use.
>
> (*CC*, p. 21n)

Haweis's earlier works on period costume had made her an authority, allowing her to analyze Chaucer's characters and to correct previous critical assumptions about the text. For example, beginning with Tyrwhitt, critics have referred to the Yeoman's "not heed" as closely cropped hair. Instead, Haweis argues, "it refers to his hood having the liripipe" ['a long pendent tail' (*OED*)] knotted around it, as there are numerous instances of such hoods worn by foresters, hunters, and others, to whom a long tail would be a nuisance, if not actually dangerous" (111–112). Modern scholars, often lacking Haweis's expertise with dress, are oblivious to the meaning of *liripipe*, although Chaucer's implied audience would not have been.

Arguing that Chaucer had a "singularly strong grasp of character" (*CC*, p. 133), Haweis attacks critics who credit the poet with superficiality:

> Mr. Bell naively points out the innocence and "ignorance of the ways of the world" which pervade the whole of the "simple Prioress's character;" but you will notice that in laughing at the cheerful nun's affectation of court manners, Chaucer never once gives her credit for very high or noble character, though he does not speak ill-naturedly. . . . She is extravagant to the last degree in feeding [to] her dogs [the most expensive of all bread], and weeping for dead mice; but nothing is said of charity to the poor, or any good works at all. She is too intent on fascinating everybody, and dressing smartly. There is sharp sarcasm in all this.
>
> (p. 23n)

From the beginning the Prioress had been problematic for scholars who refused to concede Chaucer's tone. In his edition, Bell had described this pilgrim as having "*innocent affectations*" (emphasis mine).[19] Two years earlier, Tyrwhitt had refrained from any criticism at all. Following Chaucer's description of her table manners, he noted in Old French the relevant passage from the *Roman de la Rose*, but he made no effort to connect the passages or to speculate on why Chaucer would have chosen to use almost exact wording from the French source.[20] Perhaps Haweis the first to record the Prioress's darker side.

In the controversy over Philippa Chaucer and her exact relationship to the poet, Haweis is dismissive of earlier critics, whom she felt had missed the mark. In 1857, Anna Jamieson had written of Chaucer's nine-year suit over one Philippa Picard, handmaiden to the Duchess Blanche, who was the cause of the poet's "eight year's sickness" in *The Book of the Duchess* and who ultimately became his faithful wife and companion.[21] Edward Bond had suggested in 1866 that Philippa Pan was actually Philippa Panetaria, "mistress of the pantry," an attendant on the countess of Ulster.[22] Richard Morris had claimed that Philippa was a relative or namesake of Geoffrey's, and that "he married her in the spring or early summer of 1374" (p. 5, n). Haweis scoffs:

> The old supposition that the Philippa whom Chaucer married was the daughter of Sir Paon de Roet. . . . was founded on heraldic grounds. The Roet arms were adopted by Thomas Chaucer. Then Thomas Chaucer was made (without the slightest evidence) Geoffrey's son and Philippa Roet was then made Geoffrey's wife.

She continues:

> it is. . . . much less likely that there were so many Chaucers about the Court, unconnected with each other, than that the common supposition is correct.

Philippa Pan Roet was the wife of Geoffrey Chaucer. At any rate, *until there is evidence to the contrary* [emphasis Haweis], this tradition may be fairly accepted.

(*CC*, p. 5)

Morris also erred, according to Haweis, in the description of Licurgus, King of Trace, riding into battle with "kemped heres." To Morris, the word meant "rough, shaggy," but to Haweis it means "combed," "for it seems contrary to the rule of courtesy that a noble knight should appear at a festival like a wild man of the woods" (*CC*, 48n).

Haweis's critical comments, however, are often tempered by generous praise. In her "Forewards" she writes that

Curious discoveries are still being made and will continue to be, thanks to the labors of men like Mr. F. J. Furnivall, and to many other able and industrious scholars, encouraged by the steadily increasing public interest in Chaucer.

(*CC*, n.p.)

References to these "discoveries" permeate her text. In the section on "Chaucer the Tale-Teller," Haweis writes that the poet's father was "John Chaucer, . . . a vintner in Thames Street, London," and records in her note that "Mr. Furnivall, among some of his recent interesting researches anent Chaucer, has discovered with certainty his father's name and profession," debated since the time of Speght.[23] Furnivall's assertion that "Chaucer was the son of John Chaucer, vintner, of Thames Street, London, and probably eldest son and heir, as by deed, dated June 19, 1380, and enrolled on a Hustings Roll of the City of London"[24] had appeared four years earlier under "Literary Gossip" in the *Athenæum*.

More of Haweis's comments point to Furnivall's unpublished research. Because Furnivall is known today more as an editor than as a scholar, her comments serve to augment what personal theories and interpretations have come down to us. For "Complaint of Chaucer to his Purse," she writes:

[This poem] was written, according to Mr. Furnivall, in September 1399, when Chaucer was in distress for money, and sent to Henry IV, as a broad hint, – which was at once attended to.

(*CC*, p. 103)[25]

And again,

Mr. Furnivall's ingenious suggestion, that Chaucer's penury may possibly be due to his having dabbled in alchemy . . . is borne out by the technical knowledge displayed in the Canon's Yeoman's Tale.

(*CC*, p. 103)

On "Good Counsel of Chaucer" (generally entitled "Truth"),

we have Mr. F. J. Furnivall's authority, as well as internal evidence, for believing that this pathetic little poem expresses Chaucer's feelings at the time of his expulsion from the Customs offices, the beginning of his period of misfortunes, and was written immediately after the calamity.

(*CC*, p. 104)[26]

Haweis, like Furnivall, believed that Chaucer's poverty was severe and that his "diminished income" affected his status for the rest of his life. She writes that because of the unpopularity of John of Gaunt and Chaucer's faithfulness to him, the poet was dismissed from his position at the Customs:

> He submitted to his disgrace and his poverty unmoved; and after the death of his wife Philippa . . . nothing is known of him for several years, except that he was in such distress that he was actually obliged to part with his two pensions for a sum of money in order to pay his debts.
>
> (*CC*, p. 10)

It is sad, she notes, that "during the latter years of his life, the great poet who had done so much, and lived so comfortably, should have grown so poor and harassed (*CC*, p. 11).

Chaucer for Children is the only Chaucer text that Haweis illustrated. She furnished woodcuts of all the pilgrims and color plates of several tales: "Fair Emelye," "Griselda's Marriage," "Griselda's Bereavement," "Dorigen and Aurelius," and "The Rioter." She added a portrait of Chaucer, copied from Hoccleve, and two genre paintings: "Dinner in the Olden Time" and "Lady Crossing Street." Haweis's illustrations are as carefully documented as her scholarship – MS. Reg. 2B. viii, Brit. Mus. Harl.MS.4866, Royal Coll. 20 B. 6 – a fact which sets her apart from her contemporaries. Critics commented favorably: "the strictest attention has been paid to the costumes, manners, and customs of the period"; "beautifully illustrated by large pictures painted in bright colours and by quaint woodcuts."[27] "The illustrations are especially correct, the costumes, &c, having been studied from contemporary manuscripts."[28] Miriam Youngerman Miller notes that Haweis's copious documentation of her paintings and woodcuts is "unparalleled in the world of juvenile Chaucer illustrations."[29] Haweis's printer was Edmund Evans, who in the 1860s had "established himself as the leading and best wood-block colour printer in London" (*Dictionary of National Biography*, s.v.) and his work lent to hers an immediate clout.

In 1878, three years after the first appearance of *Chaucer for Children*, the *Literary World* published its article on Chaucer, with Haweis's ideas attributed to Green. Haweis had meanwhile completed a series of commissioned articles for *Harper's Bazaar* on "women's subjects," including "Pretty and Ugly Women," "Our Poor Feet. Sandals, Clogs, and Patterns," and "The Function of a Head-Dress." That same year, Richard Morris revised his *Prologue, the Knightes Tale, the Nonne Priests Tale*, published by Clarendon, who also produced Skeat's revision of *The Pardoner's Tale, The Second Nun's Tale*, and *The Chanouns Yemannes Tale*. R. F. Weymouth produced *On "Here" and "There" in Chaucer*, a reconstruction and expansion of his work "On Early English Pronunciation," and

It happened that one day in the spring, as I was resting at the Tabard* Inn, in South-wark, ready to go on my devout pilgrimage to Canterbury, there arrived towards night at the inn a large company of all sorts of people—nine-and-twenty of them : they had met by chance, all being pilgrims to Canterbury.† The chambers and the stables were roomy, and so every one found a place. And shortly, after sunset, I had made friends with them all, and soon became one of their party. We all agreed to rise up early, to pursue our journey together.‡

But still, while I have time and space, I think I had better tell you who these people were, their condition and rank, which was which, and what they looked like. I will begin, then, with

The Knight.

GLOSSARY.
there,
valuable } A KNIGHT§ ther was and that a worthy man,   A knight there was, and that a worthy man,
          That from the tyme that he ferst bigan   Who from the time in which he first began

* A tabard was an outer coat without sleeves, worn by various classes, but best known as the coat worn over the armour (see p. 48), whereon there were signs and figures embroidered by which to recognize a man in war or tournament : for the face was hidden by the helmet, and it was easier to detect a pattern in bright colours than engraved in dark steel. So, of course, the pattern represented the arms used by him. And thus the tabard got to be called the *coat of arms*. Old families still possess what they call their coat of arms, representing the device chosen by their ancestors to 'he lists ; but they do not wear it any more : it is only a copy of the pattern on paper. A *crest* was also fastened to the helmet for the same purpose of recognition, and there is usually a 'crest' still surmounting the modern 'coat of arms.' The inn where Chaucer slept was simply named after the popular garment. It, or at least a very ancient inn on its site, was recently standing, and known as the Talbot Inn, High Street, Borough : Talbot being an evident corruption of Tabard. We may notice here, that the Ploughman, described later on, wears a tabard which may have been a kind of blouse or smock-frock, but was probably similar in form to the knight's tabard.

† People were glad to travel in parties for purposes of safety, the roads were so bad and robbers so numerous

‡ Probably all or many occupied but one bedroom, and they became acquainted on retiring to rest, at the ordinary time—sunset.

§ The word Knight (knecht) really means *servant*. The ancient knights attended on the higher nobles and were their *servants*, fighting under them in battle. For as there was no regular army, when a war broke out everybody who could bear arms engaged himself to fight under some king or lord, anywhere, abroad or in England, and was paid for his services. That was how hundreds of nobly born men got their living—the only way they could get it. This is what the knight Arviragus does in the 'Franklin's Tale;' leaving his bride, to win honour (and money) by fighting wherever he could.

The *squire* waited on the knight much as the knight did on the earl—much in the position of an aide-de-camp of the present day. The *page* served earl, knights, ladies. But knight, squire, and page were all honourable titles, and borne by noblemen's sons. The page was often quite a boy, and when he grew older changed his duties for those of squire, till he was permitted to enter the knighthood. The present knight is described as being in a lord's service, and fighting under him 'in his war,' but he was a man held in the highest honour.

Figure 2.2 Portrait of the Knight

Source: *Chaucer for Children.*

Trübner issued *A Parallel-Text Edition of Chaucer's Minor Poems* that Furnivall had previously cited. One "Professor Adams" agreed to calculate the dates of the pilgrimage, drawing from links between *The Man of Lawe's Tale* and *The Parson's Tale*.[30] And Sir Thomas Burke "recollected that the tomb of the Countess of Suffolk, the daughter of Sir Thomas Chaucer and the granddaughter of Chaucer

Figure 2.3 Fair Emelye
Source: *Chaucer for Children.*

the poet [was] still seen in good preservation at the Church of Ewelme."[31] Also in 1878, Francis Storr and Hawes Turner wrote *Canterbury Chimes: Or Chaucer Tales Retold for Children.*

Canterbury Chimes is the antithesis of Haweis's work for "little Lionel." Both Storr and Turner had graduated from Trinity College, and Storr, at least, was a considerable scholar. He published books on Francis Bacon, Milton, and French

Figure 2.4 Griselda Marriage
Source: *Chaucer for Children.*

syntax. He translated Sophocles's plays from the Greek and "The Demon of Ler-montoff" from the Russian. He wrote pedagogical articles on teaching English composition and on the use of "Cribs in Translation."[32] It is therefore surprising to find stated quite boldly in the introduction to the Chaucer text: "From erudition we have carefully abstained."[33] That fact, at least, is true:

> Liberties have necessarily been taken. Some portions have been translated, others merely paraphrased, with here and there a modern touch added.

Figure 2.5 Griselda Sorrow
Source: *Chaucer for Children.*

Mythological and astrological passages have been freely pruned. The so-called "Cook's Tale" seemed so suitable for our purpose that we have put it in the place of "Sir Thopas."

(Storr, 1898, p. vi)

Differences in spelling and pronunciation are enough to deter many grown-up people from reading Chaucer, and to children prove an insurmountable difficulty; while the occasional coarseness of the Canterbury Tales makes it an unfit book to be placed in their hands.

(Storr, 1898, p. v)

Figure 2.6 Dorigen and Arelius in the Garden
Source: *Chaucer for Children.*

As for the language,

> This is no place to discuss the problem of translation, but we may briefly submit that a mixture of prose and verse, however skillful, is jarring to all readers, and to children intolerable.
>
> (Storr, 1898, p. vi)

The text is rendered in prose.

Figure 2.7 Portrait of the Pardoner
Source: *Chaucer for Children.*

Compared with Haweis's judicious working of the introduction – the original and carefully translated couplet rimes placed side by side, words precisely glossed, and learned footnotes clarifying difficult points in the text – Storr's treatment seems bald and jarring:

In springtime, when the sweet April showers have sunk into the ground parched and hardened by the keen east winds of March, and every plant drinks the rich juices that in summer will turn to flower and fruit; when the balmy west wind blows over hill and dale and stirs the green blades in the furrows; then the sun gleams bright between the showers, and the small birds, who never close an eye the whole night long, feel the stirrings of the time and make the woods to ring, – then, in the merry springtime men's blood runs quicker in their veins and they too long to be up and doing. Some cross the seas to visit foreign shrines, but more take their way to Canterbury.

Such impoverished lines are stripped of Chaucer's every nuance; all the subtlety of the original is gone. The *Canterbury Chimes* contains no glosses, no explanatory notes. The *Graphic* commented that the book "desire[d] to afford children necessary information without hard study"[34] (or any study at all). Haweis left no extant comment.

In 1878, Haweis published *The Art of Beauty*, to the positive reviews of eager women. In it she included a passage on medieval dress, accompanied by critiques and sketches of costumes. Two years later, on August 28, 1880, the *Literary World* announced: "Mrs. H. R. Haweis is preparing a *Chaucer for Schools* founded upon her well-known *Chaucer for Children*, of which several thousand copies have been sold."[35] The *Leeds Mercury* remarked that the appeal had been "repeatedly made by schoolmasters and others engaged in tuition" that Haweis adapt Chaucer for class lessons.[36] Shortly thereafter (the letter is dated by a later hand – possibly Stephen's – "1882," but this cannot be correct because the book would have already been out for four years), Mary Eliza wrote to her mother:

> This little book is just out, so I send you a copy. It is got up in the type of the 17th century books. You see – I did all the illustrations, including the letters of the cover, & the index, (emphasis mine). . . . I have parted with the copyright of *Chaucer for Children*, which has been out 6 years, and is still selling well. I have made £235 this spring, and not before it was wanted! It sounds a large sum, but it does not go very far.
>
> (n.p.)

The positing of an older audience, one of students, freed Haweis from some of the harsher criticism that had plagued *Chaucer for Children*. "We hail with pleasure the appearance of Mrs. Haweis's *Chaucer for Schools*," the *Academy* enthused.[37] Of its critical reception in America, the *New York Times* applauded *Chaucer for Schools* for showing "both careful scholarship and an unusually appreciative critical spirit."[38]

> The present work is a delightful introduction for young people into the domestic life of the Middle Ages. The preliminary chapter on "Chaucer the Tale-Teller" is so charmingly written as to carry young people with intense enthusiasm into the reading of the "Canterbury Tales" even in the original dialect.[39]

Until well after Haweis's death, the text was among the most in demand for England's National Home Reading Union.[40]

Other critics, however, were quick to snipe. An anonymous reader for the *British Quarterly Review* notes that "a little fuller critical research and existing knowledge would have aided her" – no examples cited – "but her slips are not of a kind likely materially to reduce the value of the book in the hands of the class from whom it is meant."[41] A reader for the "School Books" section of the *Examiner* complained of the format:

> For ourselves we are inclined to think that Chaucer might well be reserved for a riper growth, albeit owning that Mrs. Haweis has done her very best to reduce him, by dint of glossary, paraphrase, and divers artifices, expurgatory and other, to the dead level of School Board understanding. In truth, the children for whose benefit the book has been planned will apparently have to keep an eye on three or four parts of the same page at once, if they are to gather the full harvest of this indefatigable lady's exegesis, and such ubiquity of vision is rare in youth, and of doubtful advantage, from a scholastic point of view, at the best of times.[42]

The *Athenæum* protested that "young persons who may – and undoubtedly many will – be led by the pleasantness of this little volume to seek a closer and fuller acquaintance with the writings of the first English storytellers, will have to *unlearn* much of what is here told them" (emphasis mine).[43]

Particularly offensive to this critic is Haweis's claim that Old [Middle] English comes easily to children, since the final *-e* is pronounced like "doggie, "horsie," and "handie." "As well might schools be told that in the Cockney 'this here' we have a relic of the þissere of early English."[44] Furthermore, Haweis had suggested that Langland's ploughman was influenced by Chaucer's pilgrim when her own time line would have made the converse true. It is the footnotes, however, that most distress this critic: Mary Eliza had asserted that the Prioress's oath "Seynt Loy" meant "by St. Louis of France," and she refuted Tyrwhitt's claim for "St. Eligius" when Tyrwhitt had actually got it right. To her elaborate description of Arcite's horse "prik[yng] endelonge the large place," the writer scoffs:

> A horse which would perform such antics might be very useful in a circus, but would be rather out of place in a duel. Evidently Mrs. Haweis takes endelonge to mean "on his hind legs," instead of simply "all along," "the whole length of."

However, he concludes: "As much as these and similar imperfections are to be regretted, they are such as can be easily remedied by an intelligent teacher." The book, therefore, is "heartily welcomed."[45]

What would students have learned from this text? Haweis's clearly laid out introduction, scholarly footnotes, and short essays following each entry make it clear what Haweis *wanted* them to learn. Was she at all realistic? Although most extant texts are, or were, owned by libraries, through an opportune bid on eBay I acquired an 1899 copy, previously owned by one Bellenelle Whitehead of New Orleans, Louisiana (n.d.), who had utilized this text in class. Because it is marked throughout, one can get a pretty fair idea of how it was presented to her. The book is in relatively poor condition and has been handled heavily. In places, its pages are taped together. On the end sheet is some illegible writing and then, "contemporary life of Chaucer's time is shown in the Prologue." On the flyleaf Miss Whitehead had written:

> You musen't [sic] mind what the authoress says in this book for as she was half dead when she wrote it, she isn't [sic] responsible for what she says.

This reference is to the in memoriam by the Rev. Haweis, where he describes Mary Eliza on her deathbed, too ill to edit the final proof sheets for the latest edition of her textbook, and himself, her afflicted husband, desperate to offer any final aid:

> She never lived to see the publication of this last complete edition of *Chaucer for Schools*, which she had been preparing and looking forward to for years. I have registered all her notes and additions, to the best of my power – it has been a task of painful and absorbing interest to me – but she could not rest until she knew that it was done.

The dedication, no doubt added postmortem, reads

> *Viro suo*
> *HUGONI REGINALDO HAWEIS*
> *Cui, quae et quails sit ipsa, id omne debet*
> *Hunc librum*
> *D.D. D.*
>
> *Uxor Grata*[46]

Such drama is a shameless fantasy staged by Hugh Reginald to save what little face he could. By 1898 his affair with Miss Emmeline Souter and the existence of their illegitimate daughter was well known, and, as previously stated, one of Mary Eliza's last acts had been to secure a divorce lawyer and disinherit him. Desperate to salvage his public reputation, but professing deep grief and total devotion, the reverend writes to "my own most precious darling": "Say a word to anyone who is about that you love me and want me as I do you. Nothing else in all the world do I want or ever have or ever shall in comparison."[47] On the night Mrs. Haweis died, her husband was, in fact, lecturing in Leeds.[48] Having exhausted her funds over the years, he hurried back to see what scraps he might still retrieve. Miss Bellenelle Whitehead never knew how much she had got it wrong.

An examination of Whitehead's text, however, reveals much about how Chaucer had been presented to her in school, and it speaks to the comments of critics who had thought that future teachers would "correct Haweis's imperfections."

This 1899 edition has been lightly marked in pencil in a hand different from the one that wrote "Property of Bellenelle Whitehead." Haweis's "Forewards" and her long introduction on "Chaucer the Tale-Teller" have not been penciled at all, nor are there marks on any of Haweis's scholarly notes. There is clear evidence, however, of the reading of some of the *General Prologue*. Whitehead has glossed certain words in the first eighteen lines (glossed, however, from Haweis's translations, placed in columns alongside the original, not from the original itself). The words "holy," Heath," "shire," and "wend" are rendered in their more familiar American equivalents: "grove," "meadow," "countries," "go." Certain of the pilgrims are scored and lines are marked: the sections on the Prioress's manners, for example, and the concern she felt for animals; the description of the Monk as a "manly man"; and the Friar's manner of hearing confession. On the Franklin's complexion, she writes "simile" on lines that are clearly nothing of the sort. She scribbled on the margins of "Notes by the Way," but not on the commentary itself.

Miss Whitehead was apparently assigned three tales – the *Knight's*, the *Clerk's*, and the *Man of Lawe's* – and her notations indicate certain pedagogical inclinations on the part of her teacher. *The Knight's Tale* was probably broken into several assignments because of the word "begin" placed at the top of a page in the middle. Whitehead repeatedly writes "chivalry," or "a tale of chivalry," indicating an emphasis on the themes of courtliness. Palamon and Arcite's promise not to hinder each other in "love" was deemed "chivalrous behavior." (The fact that this promise is promptly broken is ignored.) The eagerness of knights far and wide to attend the tournament is another example of "chivalry." "Manners and customs" were also important, and Haweis's prose description of Theseus, Hipolita, and Emelye encountering the two knights fighting in the forest was "chivalrous," as was the tone or temper of the story, for the words "humor," "humorous," and "satire" are liberally sprinkled throughout the text. Figures of speech are emphasized (apostrophe, simile, metaphor, personification) and "beautiful" passages are marked. Palamon is considered a "hearty" character and the funeral games are identified as "Greek." Haweis's notes to *The Knight's Tale* and her commentary are copious, but the student seems not to have read them.

Miss Whitehead also studied *The Clerk's Tale* as a story of wifely love and obedience.[49] All her glosses refer to Griselda, and these are "love," "humility," "self control," "piety," "industry," and "unselfishness." She marked a single phrase in Haweis's commentary: "Resignation, so steadfast and so willing." For Velma Richardson, Haweis reads this tale as "tender pathos," reflecting "the virtue of an early time, when the husband was really a 'lord and master.'"[50] But, Haweis, early champion of woman's rights, deplored this kind of wife, married as she herself was to a self-centered husband to whom she would not capitulate.[51] Had Whitehead read further, she could not have failed to see the anger Haweis unleashed on wives whose servile compliance led husbands to their "capricious outrage."

We may suppose that [Walter] was led to far greater lengths than he projected, by Griselda's eagerness to turn the second cheek to the smiter. He may have been half irritated by her servile indifference to her position and doglike attachment, and thus he gives up the complaisant attitudinizing (which does not impose on her) after his first trial of her, and the following trials are respectively more brutal and severe.

Such submission today would be more "mischievous than meritorious."

If a modern wife cheerfully consented to the murder of her children, she would probably be consigned to a maison de santé, while her husband expiated his sins on the scaffold; and if she endured other persecutions, such as Griselda did, it is to be hoped some benevolent outsider would step in, if only to prevent cruelty to animals.[52]

Mary Eliza never hid her scorn for women whom she considered to be weak. By the time of writing *Chaucer for Schools*, she was under no illusions about marital bliss. Beside the lines from Chaucer's *Man of Lawe's Tale* – "Housbondes ben alle goode, and han ben yoe, / That knowen wyues, I dar say yow no more" (p. 147) – Miss Whitehead, knowing only the fictional context for these lines, wrote "satire."

In her comments on *The Man of Lawe's Tale* Haweis refers to academic scholarship that neither students nor their teachers would have known: for example, the relationship between Chaucer and John Gower, to whom the students (but not the scholars) would have been ignorant. She rehashes the argument over whether Chaucer had borrowed the tale from the *Confessio Amantis* or from Nicholas Trivet's 1334 *Chronicle*. She traces the controversy from their supposed friendship (when Chaucer had sent Gower the *Troilus* "for correction [!]"; p. 165), to Chaucer's "unflattering" words about Gower in the *Man of Lawe's* prologue, to Gower's omitting of certain verses of praise about Chaucer upon sending the *Confessio* to Henry IV. She likens the "feud" between the two poets (there is no suggestion that the words might have been ironic) to that between William Blake and Thomas Stothard and their representations of the Canterbury pilgrims. There is no penciling on *The Pardoner's Tale*, probably indicating that this one was not read.

Haweis's Chaucer textbook – the first Chaucer textbook ever – was published by Chatto & Windus in 1881, then picked up by Scribner's in 1882, who reissued it in 1903. During her visit to New York in 1885, Haweis was told that the textbook was "largely used in American schools, having been printed in Philadelphia in a very cheap form in 1884." Chatto & Windus reprinted it in 1886, 1899, and 1900. In 1897 it was adopted for the National Home Reading Union. In 1898, the *Ipswich Journal* reported that Haweis's "books on Chaucer" had been included in Sir John Lubbeck's "Hundred Best Books."[53] Having gone through seven editions, it was last reissued in 1935. At least until 1930, it can be found listed in library bulletins and in catalogs of basic books for American high schools. For forty-four years, *Chaucer for Schools* by Mary Eliza Haweis was never out of print. Even allowing for the exaggerations of some reviewers as to the text's popularity, and for the scores of students who slept through class, failed to do their homework, or dropped out of school, *Chaucer for Children* was read and studied by scores of formative teens and future medieval scholars. Their first exposure to the poet was exactly what Haweis had laid out. Bellenelle Whitehead did not make her mark on Chaucer studies, but other, unknown readers clearly did.

In planning her textbook, Haweis had no previous models. The *Student's Chaucer*, published by Skeat in 1894, was simply a reissuing of his *Complete Works of Chaucer*, published in 1884. It contained a brief and technical introduction, an appendix of "Variations and Emendations," a glossary at the back of the book, and a complete lack of explanatory notes. It stands as a stark contrast to Haweis's work. But Haweis (possibly due to Green's influence) furnished a "Table of Historical Events" for her student readers, covering happenings in Chaucer's life and significant events "abroad." Although the chronology contains numerous errors (Gower as Chaucer's "tutor," for example, "*Langley*'s publishing of *Piers Plowman*", and *John* Van Eyck's birth in 1370), the list is interesting for setting out an old historicist approach to what Haweis believed to have been Chaucer's chronology. She conjectured that Chaucer, after completing the *Book of the Duchess* in 1369, had written what would become this first Canterbury story: *The Pardoner's Tale*. For Haweis, the death of the Duchess Blanche inspired the use of the plague background and linked the two works. In 1372, Chaucer traveled to Italy (where he possibly met Petrarch) and wrote the *Lyfe of St. Cecile*, followed by *The Clerk's Tale* in 1375, the year after Petrarch died. The third of his Canterbury stories, *The Nun's Priest's Tale*, appeared in 1381, the year of the Peasants' Revolt, and the year after the death of Bernabo Visconti, Chaucer wrote *The Monk's Tale* and included an allusion to the duke. For Haweis, the Canterbury project began in earnest in 1387, the year after Chaucer had written *The Knight's Tale* and the year he possibly made his own pilgrimage to Becket's tomb. He began both the *General Prologue* and *The Reeve's Tale* in 1388. *The Man of Lawe's Tale* was inspired by France's war with the Saracens in 1390, and the prologue was added in 1394, the year after Gower's *Confessio Amantis*. No other tales are mentioned, and scholars before or after seem not to have followed Haweis's lead. However, in constructing this chronology, Haweis shows her interest, not only in philological questions and textual emendations, but also in the evolution of Chaucer's thought.

Haweis's "Forewards" reflects the ongoing work of the Chaucer Society, which she lionized. For example, she argues that *The Parson's Tale* (apparently referring to an earlier Chaucer Society essay) was originally much less "Catholic" than it ultimately would be, had it not been

> tampered with and interpolated . . . by some unorthodox Catholic scribe. [It is] as full of Wicliffism and true Protestant feeling, as many other portions of The Canterbury Tales are full of satire against the corruption of the Church: and Chaucer may be said to have striven as hard to propagate with his pen the path of the new religious views as Albert Dürer strove with his pious pencil, long before Luther sounded the note of victory.

The interpolation theory was propounded by Hugo Simon and published in the Chaucer Society Publications, 1876, Part III.[54] Simon contended that *The Parson's*

Tale was written by three separate scribes and that the "dryer and [more] poorly written parts" (he does not specify which parts) were not Chaucer's own but were instead "interpolations" into his treatise *De Poenitentia* by an unknown individual. Furnivall had disagreed, arguing that the tale was genuine.[55] But Haweis, always eager to make Chaucer a "Protestant" if she could, sided with Simon.

After a somewhat technical discussion of meter and the various editions of the Tales useful to her book, Haweis almost casually introduces a passage which she refers to as her "new theory of Chaucer." Because Haweis is assiduous in citing both her sources and her mentors and because she is such a careful researcher herself, her claim that she has discovered "new" research – i.e., concepts distinct from those heralded by the Chaucer Society – commands attention. She writes,

> Until evidence to the contrary is forthcoming, I shall take the liberty to point out a few things which I believe may have hitherto skipped notice, but which tend greatly to link Chaucer to his time, while stimulating our interest in his writings.
>
> If these following suggestions explain and account for several peculiarities unnoticed hitherto, or unexplained, they must be accepted like every other working hypothesis until proved untrue, or until a better explanation be found.
>
> (CS, p. xv)

Haweis's first point is, surprisingly, that Chaucer's characters have "individuality, showing knowledge of human nature." To modern Chaucerians, this is a truism, but it may not have been so in Haweis's days. If it were not, when did this theory originate? In 1914, Kittredge could say with assurance, "medieval characterization was almost purely typical. Chaucer vitalized the types. . . . He submitted to the rules, and played the game as they directed, and was all the better for it."[56] He was not "original." At least until 1925 critics such as Howard Patch stated unequivocally that Chaucer relied on "types." In refuting those who had claimed that the pilgrims were "sketches" or "written upon one plan," or "reliant on Theophrastus," he argued that they were in fact based on early treatises of virtues and vices, where individuals were the extremes of their type. Haweis, however, vehemently disagreed, and she refers her readers to her analysis of certain specific characters in the *Tales*. She admonishes those "foolish" individuals who hold that Palamon and Arcite are very much alike – "proof that these persons have not read the tale" (*Chaucer for Students*, p. 89). She finds the characters to be "diametrically opposed, and never does one speak or act as the other would do" (*CS*, p. 89). Walter, of *The* Clerk's Tale, is not simply "wantonly cruel" but also "skeptic, capricious, willful, eccentric [and] spoilt," though at the end he is "honorable and generous."[57] "Yet he is so bewildered by [Griselda's] unaccustomed virtues that he could not trust their sincerity without experiments." Haweis is the first critic to use psychology in describing this man. In her mind, he is made up of too many opposing facets ever to be considered a "type."

In addition to her claim for each character's distinctiveness, Haweis argued that many were based on live models. Thirty-five years before John Manly, she asserted that "The characters in the General Prologue are no doubt all portraits." Harry Bailey is obviously the "well-known master of a well-known inn" (*CS*, p. 48, n3) and the Parson is based on the character of Wyclif. She states:

> Chaucer tells us that the ploughman was the parson's brother. Amongst those persons Wyclif found most followers, and we know that Chaucer sympathized with the Duke of Lancaster's patronage of Wyclif. It has been surmised that the parson is the great reformer himself.
>
> (*CS*, p. 46, n 3)

The Wycliffite theory, she notes, was "in the air," but she does not state who put it there.

However, it was her hypothesis that King Emeritus from *The Knight's Tale* was based on Henry of Derby, son of John of Gaunt. Haweis states:

> It is said that Henry of Derby "bore him well" at the tourney held in London in 1386. Henry was 25 in 1386, the age attributed to Emetreus. The son of a fair mother, his visage is not inconsistent: and the flattery would have been politic as well as natural.
>
> (*CS*, p. 90)

In 1916, Albert S. Cook, professor of English at Yale University, wrote: "Henry of Derby seems to have sat for the portrait of Emetreus in the *Knight's Tale*. He was no doubt more or less pitted with the smallpox or some other eruption, from which he had suffered in 1387."[58] Chaucer tones these down to "freckles." Coincidence? Possibly. Were Haweis's theories, anonymously attributed, "in the air" as so many other scholars' were? Cook's work, *The Historical Background of Chaucer's Knight*, cites many sources. *Chaucer for Schools* is not among them.

Upon the publication of *Some New Light on Chaucer* in 1926, John Manly was praised by reviewers for his belief that "behind [Chaucer's] most vital and successful sketches lay the observation of living men and women," and for collecting so much information "that his general thesis is put beyond the explanation of coincidence, which might be invoked if the question concerned only one or two of the characters."[59] According to James F. Royster, the conviction that Chaucer used material of his own experience in his poetry more fully than we have suspected cannot be easily put aside."[60] That was 1927.

But Haweis had already worked this out. She compared the characters in the *General Prologue* to the images in the paintings of Van Eyck, whose canvases were

> crowded with portraits [and] probably popular through their endless little pointed allusions, personal and political, with double meanings and hints

which we cannot now decipher. . . . It is impossible when reading any poem by Chaucer with care and vigilance, to doubt that this was so.

(*CS*, p. xvi)

Haweis was aware that much of what went into the makeup of Chaucer's poetry was forever inaccessible to readers who succeeded him and that the text itself contained references to other texts and to unannounced sources that only the immediate audience would know. She filled her notes with references to specific laws, to explanations of tournament rules, to the methods of training hawks, to astrology, coinage, mythological allusions – always with the acute realization that she had not got it all, but that Chaucer's first readers who knew so much more than we ever can, probably had.

Over a century later, Paul Strohm would write,

> Chaucer . . . celebrates the high expectations he is able to entertain of those friends as addressees of his poems – expectations of their capacity for mixed perspectives and open forms, their ability to enjoy his abrupt shifts of direction and tone, their willingness to rethink and revise prior interpretations. One has in reading these poems a sense of symbioses; a sense that Chaucer demands more of these friends and social equals than of his other possible audiences and that he gets more from them. . . . At least some of Chaucer's contemporaries did read his work attentively and with keen comprehension.[61]

Had literary criticism only developed such sophistication in Haweis's day, there is little doubt she would have endorsed it.

In "Literary Meaning and the Question of Value: Victorian Literary Interpretation," Suzy Anger argues that although "one finds only rarely [in the nineteenth century] the sort of close readings that we have come to expect in current literary analysis. . . . the formation of a number of learned societies fostered interpretative debate over meaning,"[62] eventually leading to what we know as "criticism" today. Although Haweis never gained entrance into such societies, she was, as seen in Chapter 1, both privy to and instrumental in discussions where scholars debated the legitimacy of each other's ideas and each other's words and collaborated on the meanings of new primary materials before they appeared in print. Thus these individuals – Green, a social historian, Selby, a manuscript scholar, Furnivall, a bibliographer, and Deutsch, a professional librarian – formed silent paradigms for the scholars of our modern academic world.

In addition to Chaucer's pilgrim portraits and his special communication with an implied audience, Haweis focused on Chaucer's ability to "see," or perceive with his eyes. Modern critics have commented on the poet and the medieval psychology of vision where morality or lack thereof results in perfect or imperfect sight: "seeing" is equated with "believing."[63] To my knowledge, however, Haweis is the only critic to suggest that Chaucer might literally have had defective vision. She refers to the description of the pilgrim Chaucer by the Host as being "'elvish,' or shy, 'doing no wight dalliaunce (chaffing no one), with a habit of staring on the ground, 'as if he would find a *hair*,'" (not "hare" as it is usually cited; emphasis mine). This searching for a hair on the ground is "a common habit with short sighted people," Haweis states, "and that Chaucer was shortsighted these hints, his studious ways, and the absence of description of distant scenery in his poems seems to indicate" (*CC*, p. 9). To Haweis, Chaucer was myopic, having sustained some damage to his optic nerve.

In March of 1872, Richard Liebreich, ophthalmic surgeon and lecturer at St Thomas's Hospital, spoke at the Royal Institution on "The Effects of Certain Faults of Vision on Painting with Special Reference to [J. M. W.] Turner and [William] Mulready." Included in the "crowded audience" was Mary Eliza Haweis, who wrote in her diary on March 9:

> In a very interesting lecture at the R. Institution last evening 8th March 1872, Prof. Liebreich dismayed the admirers of Turner by the alarming announcement that the strange and beautiful effects seen in his later pictures were caused not by the eccentricity of genius but by a fatal disease in the eye.

Haweis was fascinated by this theory, for a few days later she commented on an article she had written, entitled "A Physical Explanation of Turner's Later Style":

> I got an occasional note in the Echo the other day[64] about Liebreich's theory that Turner had diseased eyes, which made him see, and paint, so strangely. When I heard L. lecture, I was very much struck by the remark that as we grow older we see colours less and less distinctly owing to the probable discolouring of the crystalline lens. Have we even colour taken from us [sic] – with health and vigour, and strong feeling and clear judgement, & interest in life. . . . When our look (sic) begins to fail it is time to die.

As an artist who advocated "true color," Haweis could not imagine the world without it, and Liebreich's theory that Turner's lens grew yellow with age, caused her to speculate that the artist "gradually employ[ed] deeper and deeper hues for the purpose of getting it "right" – even without being aware of what he was doing. She sketched in her diary the "normal eye" with the lens and retina, the myopic eye, and the hypermyopic [sic] eye ("from memory"). Several years later, she turned her knowledge of optics to an understanding of Chaucer.

In 1879, she wrote in "Chaucer's Characters": "Chaucer was probably short-sighted, and his habit of looking on the ground like many myopes, which amused mine host, may have rendered more acute the penetrating glance which saw through men" (p. 40). In her notes to this passage she refers to Chaucer's

> habit of seclusion, and getting dazed with poring over his book, also like a short-sighted person, and the great absence in his writings of pictures of distant scenery, although details of the foreground are dwelt upon with very remarkable enjoyment.

The "elvish" look, or shyness, quoted by Chaucer is common with the slightly shortsighted. It is clear that Chaucer moves close up to the faces of his characters and, perhaps, as Haweis wrote for the *Echo*, his vision – the way he saw things – produced an "astonishing effect of colour" where more and more vivid hues played off one another. In an 1879 article, "Colours and Cloths of the Middle Ages," she wrote about the brilliance of color in Chaucer's close-ups and the "exact" picture he attempted to paint: "as black as any sloe," "white as morning milk," "as green as a leek." Additionally, he referred to vibrant dyes, such as "madder," "meld," and "woad" and to "metallic" colors, such as tin and "laton," as in *The Miller's Tale* and for the Pardoner's cross. Referring to French dictionaries, glosses by Skeat, paintings by Giotto, and the triptych of Matsys at Antwerp, she struggled to see just what Chaucer saw by mining nuances from his text.

By the time *Chaucer for Schools* was published, Mary Eliza Haweis was just thirty-three years old. Already she had challenged the common assumption that women (especially those who had no university education) could not produce responsible and original scholarship. She had defied authorities, spoken freely, and carved her own path through mazes of manuscripts, artifacts, and carelessly researched ideas. Drawing on her extensive knowledge of the arts and sciences as a context for Chaucer's life and works, she had become perhaps the first interdisciplinary scholar, and bolstered by the belief that Chaucer was for everyone to experience given the proper venue, she devoted the remainder of her brief life to accomplishing that goal.

Notes

1 *Academy* 10 (1876): 602.
2 *Academy* 8 (July/Dec. 1877): 542.
3 Anonymous clipping in UBC Sous Fonds; Biographical Misc. MEH 2A, folder 3, Box 31, n.p.
4 *Academy* 23 (Dec. 1876): 602.
5 *Literary World*, 28 Aug. 1886: 298.
6 David Matthews, *The Making of Middle English*, 1765–1910 (Minneapolis: University of Minnesota Press, 1999), xv.
7 Ibid., xvi.
8 Anonymous, Biog Misc MEH 2am folder 3M Box 31.
9 *Daily News*, 6 Nov. 1876: 2.
10 Ibid.
11 Anne Laurence, Joan Bellamy, Gillian Perry, eds., *Women, Scholarship, and Criticism* (Manchester: Manchester University Press, 2003), 7.
12 Bonnie G. Smith, *The Gender of History* (Cambridge: Cambridge University Press, 1996), 16.
13 *Academy* 6 (Nov. 1878): 469.
14 *Saturday Review*, p. 149.
15 Ibid.
16 Alexander Ellis, *Early English Pronunciation*. EETS, ES, 14 (London: Trübner, 1896).
17 Ibid., 679.
18 Paul G. Ruggiers, *Editing Chaucer: The Great Tradition* (Norman, OK: Pilgrim Books, 1984), 176.

19 Robert Bell, ed., *Poetical Works of Geoffrey Chaucer*, Vol. 1 (London: John Parker and Son, 1855), 82n2.

20 Thomas Tyrwhitt, *The Poetical Works of Chaucer* (London: Edward Moxon, 1852), 55n to vers 4.

21 Anna Jamieson, *Memoirs of the Loves of the Poets* (Boston: Ticknor and Fields, 1844), 80–93.

22 Edward Bond, "New Facts in the Life of Geoffrey Chaucer," *Fortnightly Review* 6 (1866): 28–29.

23 Ibid., 5n.

24 In "More News of Chaucer," *Belgravia: A London Magazine* 48 (1882): 38, written the same year as the second edition of *Chaucer for Children*, Haweis inexplicably credits the discovery of Chaucer's parentage to Walter Rye.

25 *CC*, 3 and n. Furnivall's article can be found in the *Athenæum*, 29 Nov. 1873: 698.

26 Furnivall's assertion runs counter to that of most modern critics. See *Riverside* (1088, n). There is no record showing that Chaucer sent the poem to Henry nor that the king responded with payment.

27 Miriam Miller, "Illustrations of the *Canterbury Tales* for Children: A Mirror of Chaucer's World," *Chaucer Review* 27:3 (1993): 296. See also Judith L. Fisher and Mark Allen, "Victorian Illustrations to Chaucer's *Canterbury Tales*," in *Chaucer Illustrated*, eds. William K. Finley and Judith Rosenbaum (London: British Library, 2003), 241–242. Haweis's notes on the paintings include the following sources: Vide MS. Reg 2 B. viii, and MS Imp. Lib. Paris, No. 7210, & etc., for "Dinner in the Olden Time"; Froissart's Chronicle, No. 2644, Bibl. Imp. De Paris, for "Lady Crossing Street"; Brit. Mus. Harl MS 4866 for the portrait of C; Royal Coll. 20 B.6; for the woodcuts; Royal Coll. 20 B.6; for the woodcuts: John of Gaunt; Royal MS, 14E.4, temp. ED IV for the Monk ("too late"): the Doctor, Sloane Coll. No. 1975. *Leeds Mercury*, Wed., 29 Nov. 1867, iss. 12056;" *Graphic*, 2 Dec. 1876: iss. 366. See also Velma Bourgeois Richmond, *Chaucer as Children's Literature* (Jefferson, NC: McFarland, 2004), 43. Richmond devotes several pages to Haweis's Chaucer books which she sees as thoroughly "Victorian." Haweis's "initial effort [was] that of a mother, since the eagerness and intelligence of a son inspired a confidence that children could read and respond well to Chaucer" (ibid., 36). The books contain "traditional moral values" and a [strong] moral purpose" (ibid., 45). As such, they laid a "foundation for the appreciation of a national tradition" that would be followed in other literary histories for children," such as works by H. E. Marshall, Henry Gilbert, Amy Cruse, et al. She cites that Haweis's "authorities" were writers on the history of costuming and decoration, not the famous Chaucerians of the day.

28 Richmond, *Chaucer as Children's Literature*, 296.

29 Miller, "Illustrations of the *Canterbury Tales* for Children," 296.

30 *Leeds Mercury*, 30 Jan. 1878: iss. 12420.

31 *Leeds Mercury*, 27 Feb. 1897: iss. 12444.

32 Francis Storr, *Canterbury Chimes* (London: Kegan Paul, 1898), vi. See also Francis Storr, "Teaching of English Composition," *Educational Times* 50 (May 1897): 221.

33 *CC* Kegan Paul & Co., 1878.

34 *Graphic*, 16 Nov. 1878: iss. 468, p. 1.

35 "News and Notes," *Literary World*, 28 Aug. 1880: 11.

36 *Leeds Mercury*, 4 Aug. 1880.

37 *Academy* 18 no. 451 (July/Dec. 1880): 456.

38 *New York Times*, 9 Jan. 1881: n.p.

39 Ibid.

40 Warner Snoad, "A Voice from the Talmud," *Woman's Herald* 2:77 (1893): 296.

41 *British Quarterly Review* 74:147 (July 1881): 220.

42 *Examiner*, 12 Feb. 1881.

43 *Athenæum*, 9 Apr. 1891: 489.

44 Ibid.

45 Ibid.

46 This in memoriam by the Rev. Haweis was attached to every copy of *Chaucer for Schools* after his wife's death.

47 Quoted by Bea Howe, p. 287.

48 Ironically, on that same day the *Glasgow Herald* (iss. 281) reported that Rev. Haweis's book "The Dead Pulpit," which he dedicates to "young clergy" and where he defines his beliefs as a "liberal clergyman," is one of the "new books of the week."

49 Richmond notes that *The Clerk's Tale* is in every Chaucer collection for children (*Chaucer as Children's Literature*, 39).

50 Ibid.

51 Several of Haweis's later pieces were blatantly entitled "Young Wives and Their Difficulties," *Young Woman* 4 (Sept. 1896): 417; "The Wife's Private Purse," *Women at Home* 4 (1895): 455; "Equality of the Sexes," *Review of Reviews* 4 (1873); "Insanity Considered as a Plea for Divorce," *Review of Reviews* 18 (Feb. 1898): 174; and "Married Woman's Property Act," *Spectator Archive* 24 (Mar. 1883): 25.

52 Haweis, "Married Women's Property Act."

53 *Ipswich Journal*, 10 Dec. 1898: iss. 9683, n.p. Lubbert first drew up his list in 1886, which he periodically revised. The list led to the Great Books Movement.

54 Hugo Simon, "Chaucer as a Wicliffite: An Essay on Chaucer's Parson and *Parson's Tale*," *Chaucer Society Essays* 1 (1876): 232–243.

55 Ibid.

56 George Lyman Kittredge, *Chaucer and his Poetry* (Cambridge: Harvard University Press, 1946), 29. These lectures were reprinted from 1914.

57 Rev. A. W. Reed, "Some New Light on Chaucer," *RES* 4 (1928): 217.

58 Rev. James F. Royster, "Some New Light on Chaucer," *MLN* 42:4 (1927): 251.

59 Ibid.

60 Ibid., p. 255.

61 Paul Strohm, *Social Chaucer* (Cambridge: Harvard University Press, 1989), 75.

62 Jennifer Holberg and Marcy H. Taylor, "Pedagogy: Cultural Approaches to Teaching Literature and Language," *Composition and Culture*, 4:1 (2004): 29.

63 See, for example, Angela Lucas, "The Mirror in the Marketplace: Januarie through the Looking Glass," *Chaucer Review* 33 (1998): 123–145; Linda Tarte Holley "Medieval Optics and the Framed Narrative in Chaucer's 'Troilus and Criseyde'," *Chaucer Review* 21 (Summer 1986): 26–44. See also Peter Brown, *Chaucer and the Making of Optical Space* (New York: Peter Lang, 2007); Suzanne Conklin Akbari, *Seeing through the Veil: Optical Theory & Medieval Allegory* (Toronto: University of Toronto Press, 2006).

64 Cited by *Leeds Mercury*, 14 Mar. 1872: iss. 10585.

3 Mary Eliza Haweis and *The Miller's Tale*

The sentiments of Chaucer are often more indelicate than the lowest vulgarity, the most boorish rusticity will now be found to authorize. And although in paraphrases like the [*Miller's Tale*], the gross as well as the obsolete phrases of his language may be softened; so interwoven is the tenor of his stories with indecency, that no subterfuge can be devised by which that blot may be absolutely obliterated.

> Anonymous, 1791

Such tales shall be left untold by me.

> "Chaucer," John Dryden, from Preface to the Fables,
> Henry Craik, ed. English Prose, 1916

[*The Miller's Tale*] is one of the most completely funny tales ever conceived.

> Mary Eliza Haweis[1]

The archives of the University of British Columbia Library contain a manuscript written in a small, tidy hand, in black ink on cream-colored paper, with footnotes in red. It is one of seven similar manuscripts in an acid-free folder in a gray Hollinger archives box. It was written, polished, and made ready for a publication that did not come about. It is likely never to have been read. Entitled "The Story of Alison," it begins, "Once upon a time there dwelt in Oxford a rich old fellow who took in boarders. . . ."[2]

Although most of the pilgrims "loughe[d] and pleyde" after hearing *The Miller's Tale*, nineteenth-century audiences did not find it so funny. William Lipscomb's turn of the century modernization of the *Tales* omitted those of the Miller and the Reeve.[3] Wordsworth eliminated the tale as well, even though he had once sat "comfortably" around the fire with Dorothy while she read it to him.[4] In *Tales from Chaucer Told for Young People*, published in 1833, Charles Cowden Clarke struck the tale without comment.[5] But in his 1896 edition of *The Riches of Chaucer*, he wrote to his audience that *The Miller's Tale* is "good of [its] kind, but not such as you would care to hear, so I will leave [it] out."[6] In 1878 it was omitted without explanation, along with the Reeve's tale, from Storr and Turner's *Canterbury Chimes*. In his 1845 *Cabinet Pictures of English Life*, John Saunders noted that the story was "one of Chaucer's richest and broadest" and the "laugh at its conclusion [was] loud and long,"[7] but he gave not a detail of elaboration.

Saunders' *Miller's Tale* reads as follows: "For I will tell a legend and a life / Both of a carpenter and of his wife,' &c. when he himself was interrupted by the Reeve."[8] In his edition of 1889, he boldly included the tale (or rather the "tale") heavily excerpted at the back of the book, along with that of the Reeve, Merchant, and Shipman. Skeat, hoping to exonerate the poet from an obvious "lapse," suggested that the death of Chaucer's wife Philippa in 1387 was responsible for the "coarseness" of *The Miller's Tale* and others, but he does not explain why this would be so.[9] As John Urry had declared in 1721, commenting on Chaucer's own caveat ("Turn over the leef. . . .): Reader, you know what you are to expect; read or forbare!"[10]

No nineteenth-century version of *The Canterbury Tales* could be counted on to include the story as Chaucer had written it – or to include it at all. In a table labeled "[Chaucer] Tales Selected for Collection" in her *Chaucer as Children's Literature*, Richmond lists various nineteenth-century versions of *The Canterbury Tales* that include *The Miller's Tale* (and others). She cites its inclusion only in William Calder's "very brief synopsis" of the offensive work in 1892. Haweis's compilation was reported not to have contained the tale.[11]

It was not editors and translators alone who felt obliged to denigrate the story to their respective readers. Men of letters weighed in as well. To authors like Lord Byron and Kenelm Henry Digby, the tale was "obscene"; Walter Scott considered it "extremely gross"; for Lowell, it was a "smooch" that showed up here and there in Chaucer's work. Clough described it as "rude" and "indelicate" and suggested that it be ignored. Cardinal Wiseman found it morally corrupt, and Adolphus William Ward, noting that *The Miller's Tale* was told in a churlish manner, concluded "of which manner, the less said the better."[12]

Given this context, it is not surprising that such few analyses of *The Miller's Tale* as appeared in the 1800s chose cautious and narrow theses.[13] British scholars proudly analyzed the *Knight's*, the *Man of Lawe's*, and the *Clerk's* tales, confident that these works were safe. Issues ranged widely and were faced squarely. But *The Miller's Tale* proved a minefield of danger. Those scholars who hesitantly approached it (possibly hoping to reclaim some respectability for the work) chose not its fabliau elements but its sacred ones. Haweis's own reading would be the exception.

Popular for general scrutiny was the "curious Night Charm," uttered by the Carpenter in response to the disappearance of Nicholas into his room upstairs.

> Lord Jhesu Crist, and seynte Benedyht,
> Blesse this hous from every wikked wight,
> Fro nyghtes verray, the white Paternostre
> When wonestow now, seynte Peteres soster.[14]

Critics raised various issues: the meaning of the word "verray" in the phrase "nyghtes verray," also glossed as "nyghtes mare"; the choice of the phrase, "seynte petres soster" – why not his "brother"? In 1850, William J. Thoms asked readers of *Notes & Queries* for some explanation of this passage and got several tentative returns, including one from Daniel Rock, who suggested that St. Peter's sister was drawn from the story of St. Petronilla in *The Golden Legend*.[15] Thoms's ensuing article "Chaucer's Night-Spell" (1878) recounted the state of present criticism and concluded that the charm "reminded him" of "The Little Creed" to the Virgin and other medieval prayers in common use in England. In a follow-up "Note on the White Paternoster" (1878), Evelyn Carrington extended the geographical range of these Paternoster prayers to include France, Italy, Germany, and Sardinia.[16] There is no mention of lusty wives, hot coulters, or shot-windows in any of these highly restricted pieces.

The "Angelus ad Virginem" that Nicholas sang to Alison also sparked debate. Tyrwhitt had tentatively suggested that it was the "Ave Maria."[17] However, an anonymous article appearing in 1882 printed a copy of the words and "original music" discovered in the BM Arundel 248 by Rev. H. Combs, and proved it to be a dialogue between the Virgin and Gabriel at her Immaculate Conception. The article, entitled "The Song of Chaucer's Clerk of Oxenford, 'Angelus ad Virginem,'" seems oblivious to the tale's salacious plot. But Tyrwhitt fixed on the description of Arundel 248 and its probable origin, noting that the song was in wide circulation about fifty years before Chaucer's time. The poet chose it for its popularity, the author claims, because it was the "best representative of the religious hymn or song or lay then prevalent."[18] For modern critics, Chaucer's motives were not so pure.[19]

In one of her "at home" speeches (see Chapter 4) delivered in 1890, Haweis observed that

> Many, even of the highly cultured classes still hardly realize Chaucer's unique history & historical position. When they don't flee him as a regular Bogey, they are apt to regard him as a mere old world poetaster, too "difficult" to read for pleasure & too dull for profit, whilst his "funning" is considered too coarse at any rate for ladies & this from people who say that they like Shakespeare and don't see anything coarse about him![20]

Enticed by Chaucer's "funning," Haweis published a variety of pieces on *The Miller's Tale* between 1877 and 1886. "The Story of Alison" was written sometime before 1878. Attached to the story is an analysis ("Notes by the Way") directed toward an audience of children and their mothers or tutors. Next came two articles: "Chaucer's Characters" and "Colours and Cloths of the Middle Ages." The *Routledge World Library Series* (1887), edited by her husband, contained her new adaption of the work, this time with *The Miller's Tale* followed by a completely new "Afterwards" for adult readers. Arguably, Haweis wrote more on *The Miller's Tale* than any other Victorian writer.

One can probably never know the circumstances surrounding Haweis's initial rendering of *The Miller's Tale*. At the top of the first manuscript page in the fascicle lurks a single clue. Written in faded ink to the right of the title are the words "Mrs. Haweis/16 Welbeck St. W" – the address of Haweis and her husband after their marriage in 1868. By 1878, the Haweises were living in "Amber House"

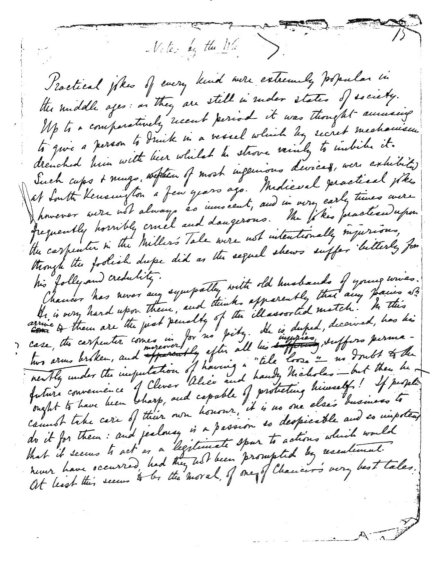

Figure 3.1 The Miller's Tale

Source: University of British Columbia Sous Fonds 5–7 Box 23.

on St. John's Wood Road. This information places the story earlier, somewhere during the ten-year period when Storr and Turner had chosen publicly to omit it. Haweis had recorded in a diary entry for March 5, 1876, that she was working on a "Chaucer book," title unspecified. *Chaucer for Children* was first published that next year, and "The Story of Alison" seems originally crafted for that anthology. Yet, Haweis ultimately omitted the Miller completely from *Chaucer for Children* and left no space where the portrait or tale could have fit. Her correspondence with Chatto & Windus on its publication contains no reference to that work.[21]

Nevertheless, Haweis worked diligently over "The Story of Alison." Her text includes 154 lines of Chaucer's original in parallel columns with her own careful translations. She added numerous explanatory notes, including glosses of "clerk" (Haweis rarely missed the opportunity to write negatively of the Catholic Church), "child," "meath," "laudes," "underspore," and "pointe-devise." She described medieval Oxford and Oseney Abbey, "where the carpenter probably found constant employment" (*SA*, p. 3). She commented on the carpenter's oath to St. Frideswide, noting its particular significance to the story line:

> the many local allusions [in the tale] prove Chaucer's familiarity with Oxford. The only church dedicated to the saint [Frideswide] in England is the Priory (now Christ Church) there: the oldest church in Oxford. The oath too "by St. Thomas," used frequently by Chaucer in this tale, was to St. Thomas of Kent, to whom the church at St. Osney is still dedicated.
>
> (*SA*, p. 6)

Ever a connoisseur of fashion, she noted that Alison's "smok" was high-necked and short-sleeved, and that the patterns on Absolon's shoes resembled the Gothic windows in St. Paul's. She clarified Nicholas's "augrim-stones" as "counters," "augrim" being a "a corruption of algorithm, the Arabian word for numeration" (*SA*, p. 2). She referred to William Lambarde's "Topographical Dictionary for the founding of the Abbey at Oxford" and to Henry Morley's *First Sketch of English Literature* (1873)[22] on the subject of religious plays. She remarked upon the unusual nature of Nicholas's private room in the carpenter's "inn," since "a room exclusively of one's own was an exceptional luxury. Among the lower classes at least, several beds in one room, even in private houses, was the rule" (*SA*, p. 1).

Haweis's transformation of Chaucer's tale is ingenious. As she made clear in *Chaucer for Schools*, she was uncommonly well versed in the various Chaucer editions and manuscripts, and she moves easily from one to another. In her "Forewards," for example, she observes that Morris preferred the Harleian MS. 7334, collated with the Lansdowne MS. 851, in the case of corrupt readings of the former. She adds: "This method I have followed when I have ventured to change a word or sentence, in which case I have, I believe, invariably given my authority" (*CS*, p. xii). The rewriting of Chaucer's original, as we have seen, was distasteful to Haweis, who had written glowingly of the poem's beauty and stateliness. Still, the language of *The Miller's Tale* was not for Victorian children and some transformation was advised.

Haweis's story is deceptively naïve. It tells of two "children" who wanted to play with one another. One of these, a "nice" girl named Alison, was married to an old, jealous carpenter, and the other, Nicholas, a charming student, was studying astrology and living in the old man's house. Looking for amusement, the two decided "that it would be great fun to play some clever trick upon [the husband] the carpenter . . . so as to get rid of him, and have some time to themselves" (*SA*, p. 5), and so they fabricated their "little plan" of Noah and the flood. Another youngster eager to play, but only with Alison, was Absolon, a parish clerk who was "not always liked." Contrary to the others, he was "squeamish" (of what, Haweis does not say), despised "vulgar jokes," and could be most disagreeable when he chose. He came to sing under the bedroom window, annoying both Alison and John. Learning from Nicholas about the oncoming "flood," the carpenter made large tubs for the roof so that he, Nicholas, and Alison could sit there and be saved. Soon John began to snore; the two friends climbed down to play, "and fine fun they had" (*SA*, p. 10). Absolon happened by as well, and, sticking his head into the bedroom window, asked Alison for a kiss, his love for her having made him so miserable that he could not "eat [his] dinner." Craftily she went to the window and "banged a broom into his face" (emphasis mine). Furious, he ran to the blacksmith, and, borrowing a hot coulter, raced back to the window. This time, it was Nicholas "who rashly opened the window," and Absolon hit him so fiercely that he "brought off whole passages of skin" from unspecified places. Nicholas yelled, "water!"; John fell from the window; and "everybody had a good laugh."

The "laughing" in the tale, however, is double-edged. To the initiated reader, Haweis's references to "play," "enjoy[ing] oneself," and "amusing themselves til ever so late" contain an odd ambiguity, as does Absolon's unexplained "squeamish[ness]" and his abhorrence of "vulgar jokes." Despite Absolon's "fussiness" and dislike of foolery, his reaction to Alison's response for a "friendly kiss" seems excessive:

> She opened the lattice a little way and banged a broom into his face – which made him so dreadfully cross, and startled him so that he did not know what to do with himself for rage (*SA*, p. 11). . . . Now this silly Absolon was so angry, he bit his lips for rage. He cleaned his mouth and rubbed it with dust, with sand, with straw, with cloth, with chips, but he could not forget Alison's rudeness. He did not care a bit about her now, and nearly cried with spite.
>
> (*SA*, p. 12)

Even the jesting of his friend Gervase, the blacksmith, could not calm him, for he "had more tow on his distaff [more business to attend to] than Gervase knew." Haweis does not elaborate on these events, but at a later date, and for a different audience, she would be less discreet.

Chaucer's tale lacks an apparent moral, but Haweis's rendition does not, and she reinforces it at every turn: husbands who jealously restrain their wives must be punished. This obvious addition of an overt lesson did not seem to trouble Haweis because "all of [Chaucer's] merriest stories [have] a fair moral; even those which are too coarse for modern taste" (*CC*, p. xii). While Chaucer had merely asserted that John "heeld [his wife] narwe in cage" (l. 3225), Haweis insisted that he was so jealous of his wife that he would "scarcely let anyone speak to her"; he would "half kill" her if she got out of his sight." Moreover, he is stupid to a fault. She glosses:

> What can be more ridiculous than the conduct of this ignorant and super-
> stitious old fellow, dupe as he was all the while of the scholar's despised

cleverness? The mode of rousing a man [Nicholas] whom he supposes to be in a fit or trance, the various incongruous charms he uses, winding up with the "nightspell," supposed to be efficacious against nightmare, is infinitely amusing and characteristic.

(SA, p. 7n)

He was fit to be tricked and mocked "for all his jealous keeping of his wife" (*SA*, p. 14).

Having completed a suitable children's story, Haweis preceded to explain it as a "joke." Although familiar with the term "fabliaux," she found it more suitable for *The Friar's Tale*. ("Mr. Wright conjectures that [*The Friar's Tale*] was translated from some old fabliaux" [*SA*, p. 64n]). To the Victorian audience, this word seems to have meant "a metrical tale, belonging to the early period of French poetry; a tale with "broad humor" (*OED*, s.v.). In her list of "Principal Authorities Consulted in this Book," Haweis lists both Le Grand's (1840). and Barbazan's, *Fabliaux et contes* (1808). These contain narratives ranging from homely anecdotes to knightly quests, and include such stories as "Aucassin and Nicolette" and "Griselda," not fabliaux in any modern sense of the word.

Because any sort of Victorian exegesis of *The Miller's Tale* is uncommon and because a child's rendition is unparalleled, Haweis's comments following the tale, her "Notes by the Way," are worth scrutiny:

> Practical jokes of every kind were extremely popular in the middle ages: as they are still in ruder states of society. Up to a comparatively recent period it was thought amusing to give a person to drink in a vessel which by secret mechanism drenched him with beer whilst he strove vainly to imbibe it. Such cups & mugs, of most ingenious device, were established at South Kensington a few years ago.

"Puzzle jugs," popular as Victorian toys, seem a long way from suitors and brooms, but Haweis is appealing directly to children. The mechanisms of medieval jokes, she admits,

> were not always so innocent, and in very early times were frequently horribly cruel and dangerous. The jokes practiced upon the carpenter in the *Miller's Tale* were not intentionally injurious, though the foolish dupe did as the sequel shews suffer bitterly for his folly and credulity. Chaucer has never any sympathy with old husbands of young wives. He is very hard upon them, and thinks apparently that any pains wh/ arrive to them are the just penalty of the ill assorted match.

In her later years, Haweis wrote articles on husbands and wives and on how the wife might best "survive." Husbands who "guarded their wives," however justified their intentions might have been, came in for sharp rebuke. John shows kindness both toward Alison and Nicholas, but with Haweis John comes in for no pity.

He is duped, deceived . . . and moreover after all his injuries suffers permanently under the imputation of having a "tile loose" – no doubt to the future convenience of Clever Alice and handy Nicholas – but then he ought to have been sharp, and capable of protecting himself! If people cannot take care of their own honour, it is no one else's business to do it for them: and jealousy is a passion so despicable and so impotent that it seems to act as a legitimate spur to actions which would never have occurred, had they not been prompted by resentment. At least this seems to be the moral, of one of Chaucer's very best tales.

(SA, p. 15)

The poet himself might have been surprised to see what he wrote!

Haweis's treatment of *The Miller's Tale* is exceptional. Not only had she turned a taboo story into one appropriate for adolescents, but she had also managed to include morals and even reminders of proper manners. Absolon is an unwelcome visitor to the carpenter's hostelry; his arrivals were neither "expected" nor agreeable: "[he] treated his friend's house as if it was a hotel, making [his] calls, transacting business about the town, and coming and going at all hours to suit [his] own convenience" – prohibited, according to *The Essential Handbook of Victorian Etiquette*.[23] Moreover, he conducted his visits "between 2 & 3" in the morning, which Haweis found disturbing: during Chaucer's time, she glosses, "it was usual to rise at 6, and not uncommon to rise at four, but three was rather nocturnal for a neighborly visit."[24] Finally, Absolon asked for a kiss, "which he had no business to ask for," and his "impertin[ence in coming] so early that it was still quite dark & to want to talk to her," leads Alison to formulate her plan (Story of Alison, p. 11). Only once does Absolon follow strict Victorian courtesy: he "cough[ed] gently" before approaching Alison at the shot-window. Haweis remarks: "It was considered polite and enjoined by etiquette, to cough before summoning the friend visited; in order to warn him of your approach, lest thro' open door or window his private conversation not be overheard"(SA, p. 12, n 2). Yet, even this formality did not profit him: "ne hadde [he] for his labour but a scorn."

The principal characters of *The Miller's Tale* are clearly unsuited for an audience of children, so Haweis carefully changed them. To Alison's portrait, she added "nice," and "almost a child in years." She removed "wylde," "cokewold," "wench," and any suggestion that Alison might "lay with a lord." Haweis's Nicholas, who does not catch Alison "by the queynte" or hold her "hard by the haunchebones," is seen as "clever" and "useful"; he had many friends and a pleasant voice. Still, for the initiate, Chaucer's original version will occasionally resound: "'*Handy Nicholas' had many ways of making himself useful*"; "*he understood love philters* [seductive potions], *and all sorts of secrets*" (emphases mine). Stripped of its salacious context, the line hangs like a dead branch. And there is the ominous "broom," to which we shall return, and Absolon's inordinate rage when he encounters it.

In adapting this tale for children, Haweis made extraordinarily meticulous choices. She understood the texts intimately and had found the scarce translations unsuitable. And she was adamant about letting Chaucer speak in his own voice. The resulting story contains lines quoted directly from Chaucer's text and additional passages of reverberations. Haweis delighted in the poet's details, his metaphors, and his maxims. Even in paraphrase she managed to keep them, and she retained Chaucer's dialogue whenever she could. The result is a captivating story of memorable characters "funning" in a pseudo-medieval world.

Haweis's creation of Alison is extraordinary for its time. First off, she fits none of the popular Victorian stereotypes for females. She is neither a mother, a spinster, a daughter, nor a woman of fantasy. She is not a "fledgling" who has been misunderstood, nor a dutiful female with sickly parentage. She is not a child "naturally naughty and so in need of reform . . . or pure . . . require[ing] protection from evil influences."[25] Edith Lazaros Honig remarks that after the publication of *Alice in Wonderland*, "writers felt free to depict little girls who could be independent, aggressive, and even rebellious."[26] But Alison is not a "little girl"; she is a wife, one whose world is not defined by a mother or by a man. Unlike Lewis Carroll's heroine, she does not mature along the way; she learns nothing; she is not punished; and at least to Haweis's mind, she will do it again. John's reputation for having a "tile lose" was to the "future convenience" of Alison and Nicholas. Richmond observes: "Among the many efforts to present Chaucer for children, [Haweis's] is the most complex and advanced."[27]

The completion of "The Story of Alison" did not end Haweis's fascination with *The Miller's Tale*. By the middle of the nineteenth century many women writers had turned to journalism, adding fashion and domesticity to the more "weighty" subjects of science, religion, and philosophy intended for men. Such women wrote for a new type of "family magazine": education and entertainment directed toward females. As Jennifer Phegley notes, "family magazines provided women with a mainstream forum that invited them to develop their own ideas about literature and to engage in the kinds of critical discussions from which they were typically excluded."[28] By 1879, Haweis had returned to *The Miller's Tale*, writing a "review" for *University Magazine*, where her essay on "Chaucer's Characters"[29] mingled with such pieces as "Anglo-Indian Poets," "Novels of Richard Blackmore, "Distressed Gentlewomen," "Fashionable Crazes," and "Fairy Superstitions in Donegal." For a magazine whose readers consisted mostly of females, Haweis has refashioned her story line. The former Alison, "almost a child in years," has grown into "a women for all times."

Unlike earlier male critics who had tended to omit *The Miller's Tale* from their works or to warn off any would-be explorers, Haweis obviously expected her audience to be thoroughly familiar with the story as originally written. She is frank about the lovers' tryst and never suggests that the two want simply to "play" with children their own age, as she does in "The Story of Alison." Here Alison is a "naughty girl" without "morale" whose assignation will, and should, continue long after the tale is done: John is suffering from mania – an imputation he "labours" under ever after, no doubt to the future convenience of "hende" Nicholas and clever Alice. Nicholas, so excited over Absolon's return that he forgets his wit, "encounters him and his red-hot coulter so warmly that he loses his head" and shouts for "water." With her adult audience, Haweis has more room to roam.

Throughout the essay, Haweis reveals surprising insights into Chaucer's text that seem to have vanished and then been discovered anew by more modern critics to whom she was not even a name. For example, the portrait of Alison, she notes, is loaded with "pleasant imagery of country life," serving to underscore both her prettiness and her frisky, "flickering" nature.

> All flowers and fruits are pressed into her service, and country drinks and occupations, and country beasts and birds: a whole year of sweet scenes come before the mind, of wilding woods, and tended orchards, and hedges full of berries and young birds.
>
> ("C's Char.," p. 31)

She directs the reader to the words "wesil," "morne mylk," "perjonete tree," the wool of a "wethir," a "swalwe chitering on a berne," and a kid or calf "frolicking behind its mother" ("C's Char.," pp. 30–31). Chaucer ends with the primroses and heartsease in Alison's hair, Haweis notes, "under the necessity of ceasing her praises somewhere" ("C's Char.," p. 31).

Paul E. Beichner and Charles Muscatine, writing in 1943 and 1957, respectively, carry this pastoral theme further: "by associating Alison with things of the country, [Chaucer] render[s] the unseemly manner of her rejection of Absolon plausible. Alison and Absolon, one country-bred and the other citified, are foils for each other."[30] And Muscatine: "Alison's country images, weasel, colt, piggesnye, etc., show her as 'a delectable little animal, who is not to be won by a protracted, artificial wooing.' The 'morne milk,' 'wolle . . . of a wether,' 'hoord of apples, contribute to more than one strand' of imagery making up her portrait."[31] Haweis is unusual among her contemporaries for the close attention she pays to the text, pondering individual words, scrutinizing with a painter's eye:

> These [portraits] are but sketches, but by no means slight or superficial. Every line, like a drawing by Landseer or Rubens, bears the value of the master's past years of thought and labour, and carries more meaning than twenty by a meaner artist.
>
> ("C's Char.," p. 34)

In "The Story of Alison" Oseney is but a name, but in "Chaucer's Characters," Oseney ("Osenay," "Oseyene") was more than a convenient three-syllable rhyme for "pleye" and "Saterday." In *Chaucer at Oxford and Cambridge*, J.A.W. Bennett describes Oseney as being associated with bullbaiting and bookmaking; it was carefully chosen as a town "where there would always be jobs for a carpenter, including the building or repair of houses on the abbey's city properties; and there would always be a need for timber, if only for firewood."[32] Thus, John had ample reason to go there.

Haweis, too, sees Oseney as a place where John would have derived his wealth, but she hints at another premise, far in advance of her time: that the saints' names associated with Oseney were not randomly selected but were carefully chosen for their relevance to the story line. Modern critics would simply assume that such would be the case, but in Haweis's time, the notion was novel:

> Alison's oath, "By St. Thomas of Kent," refers to Becket, to whom a church near Oseney is dedicated. John's invocation of St. Frideswide is also curiously appropriate; for the only church in England dedicated to this Saxon saint is the Priory at Oxford (now Christ Church), the oldest church in Oxford, then held in great repute.
>
> (p. 31)

In "Three Notes on The Miller's Tale" (1963), Ruth H. Cline argues that "several subjects of interest which have not been fully studied" in that tale are the "local saints," including St. Thomas and St. Frideswide.[33] The church of St. Thomas, she asserts, "was probably built between 1187 and 1191 by Oseney Abbey and became the parish church immediately after its completion."[34] The priory of St. Frideswide was "the richest church in Oxford." Mrs. Haweis, had asserted as early as 1883, that Chaucer's words are always exact and that names "are to some extent a chronicle of their time and an index of the manners of the age":[35] an index to social history.

> Like the subject of a Pre Raphaelite painting, Haweis's adult Alison is erotic, passionate, and wild, inhabiting a medieval world of Victorian invention: All flowers and fruits are pressed into her service, and country drinks and occupations, and country beasts and birds: a whole year's sweet scenes come before the mind, of wilding woods, and tended orchards, and hedges full of berries and young birds, the clink of the pail as the milking maidens saunter home through meadows powdered with flocks: and apple-hards brought in with singing by the maids and boys: a river, boat-laden – may be the Thames itself – in sight, beside whose brink the young men practised archery – with glimpses of a mast beyond the sunset.
>
> ("C's Char.," p. 30)

Alison herself is a "primerole and a "piggesneyde." Haweis's Chaucer the "nature poet," rounds out his sketch by "crowning her fair hair with primroses and hearts-ease, under the necessity of ceasing her praises somewhere" ("C's Char.," p. 31).

For Mary Eliza Haweis, Alison's world was Chaucer's world as well. In her introduction to *Chaucer for Schools* and *Chaucer for Children*, she wrote that "when Chaucer walked in those streets [of London], the birds sang over his head, and the hawthorne and primrose bloomed where now the black smoke and dust would soon kill most green things" (*CS*, p. 7).

> When the month of May arrived . . . everybody, rich and poor, [got] up very early in the morning to gather boughs of hawthorn and laurel, to deck all the doorways in the street, as a joyful welcoming of the sweet spring time. . . . [Chaucer] also tells us how he loved to rise up at dawn in the morning, and go into the fresh fields to see the daisies open.
>
> (*CS*, p. 4)

Such a vision of the poet, pure fantasy to the modern reader, was emblematic to Victorian eyes, for "London [was] oh, so much prettier [then]" with its streets "full of fragrance, its meadows "within a walk" away.

By the late nineteenth century, half of the six million women in England, including Haweis herself, had joined the workforce. Appropriately enough, the adult Alison also holds a job. Her husband ran an inn, "probably for the convenience of the Oxford students," ("C's Char.," p. 31) where Alison, like many Victorian women in small family partnerships, worked behind the scenes, in retailing, bookkeeping, correspondence, dealing with clients, and arranging details. Alison served as "hostess" (the irony is muted here), her "beauty and civility" helping to attract guests. But she was also a "tradeswoman, and may have kept her husband's books, received and entered orders," thus filling her husband's coffers ("C's Char.," p. 31). Haweis describes "the pretty, busy creature singing at her work, but by no means unconscious of the approving glances while she does it" ("C's Char.," p. 30).

No longer concerned with instructing young children, Haweis is free to cast Alison as "wild" and "naughty," with a "laxity of morale still more common even then than now" ("C's Char.," p. 34). She "loved" Nicholas but, in a strange departure from Chaucer's text, was not totally adverse to Absolon; his "influence in the Abbey" was seen as "status," adding to his acceptability as a lover. Haweis even speculated, unlike Chaucer, that Alison possibly "felt awkward before so superior a person, and scorned him with a little chagrin." Were it not for Nicholas, she might have encouraged the parish clerk, "for without liking a man it is possible to like his homage, and we must suppose that he was not silly enough to pursue a woman who had made him feel that he was distasteful" ("C's Char.," p. 32). Alison is also capable, "like unprincipled maids of later date [of] us[ing] one lover to conceal another" ("C's Char.," p. 33). A "coquette," her amorous intentions could be capricious.

Although the format and audience of "Chaucer's Characters" differs from that of "The Story of Alison," the one helps to explain the other. "Chaucer's Characters" draws heavily from the earlier unpublished work, suggesting that that text was at hand while Haweis was writing her review. Sometimes Haweis borrows direct passages, as when she remarks that the carpenter's "mania – an imputation he labour[ed] under ever after, [served] no doubt to the future convenience of hende Nicholas and clever Alice" ("C's Char.," p. 33). Still, the later version is curiously less academic. "The Story of Alison," as we have seen, is heavily footnoted, while "Chaucer's Characters" is not. In the latter work, for example, Haweis remarks only that Chaucer himself might have been present at miracle plays held in Oxford, since "Alison's admirer Absolon figured as Herod" ("C's Char.," p. 31). But in "The Story of Alison" she explains at length that

religious plays were a very old institution. They were somewhat like those at Armmergau now. The scaffold on which they were performed was erected in a broad street, or a field: and Absolon as a church official took part in them, Chaucer says, in the character of Herod. These plays formed part of the regular religious instruction of the populace, & were regarded in all solemnity. They ceased in about 1580. See Morley's "First Sketch of English Literature."
("C's Char.," p. 4)

Henry Morley's work describes the miracle plays in Chester and London and confirms Haweis's careful research. Drawing from "a twelfth-century ms., found in the library town of Tours," he recounts stage directions and stage space, and remarks upon the "outdoor scaffolding, attached to the church, [which] trampled the graves in the churchyard."[36] He notes that

> as miracle plays increased in popularity, the parish clerks occupied themselves much with the acting of them. Chaucer's jolly Absolon [sic], of whom we are told that "sometimes to shew his lightness and maistrie / He playeth Herod on a scaffold high," was a parish clerk.

The comparative treatment of miracle plays points up the vastly different audiences for whom Haweis's two pieces on *The Miller's Tale* were intended. Women who instructed their children in Chaucer's rime scheme and metrics were expected to have a substantial backup library for enrichment; female readers of the *University Magazine* were of a different sort. They wanted story line and light entertainment, and, as a versatile writer, Haweis reformulated her script.

"The Story of Alison" makes short shrift of the little town of Oseney; children would hardly care. But the audience of "Chaucer's Characters" would have had antiquarian interest. The town, noted in Baedeker's guide as a "fashionable" side trip from Oxford, is described there in picturesque detail:

> Osney [sic], frequented by the carpenter, still exists as a crowded suburb of Oxford – a mass of dingy streets and workmen's houses which have sprung up during the last twenty years. But in Chaucer's day Osney was a tract of land well outside the city to the north-west, watered by the Thames and broken into islands by its numerous little arms or branches, one of which islands was from Henry I's time up to the Reformation the site of the Abbey of Osney, "an abbey of Augustine canons, founded by Robert d'Oilli, which soon grew to wealth and importance, its abbot being possessed of a seat in Parliament."[37]

Using an unattributed source, Haweis noted that the Abbey walks, shaded by fine elms (whose beauty was alluded to by Leland just before the dissolution), served for recreation to the Oxford folk ("C's Char.," p. 31).

Oseney, with its tree-lined walks and its background of medieval ruins, provided the perfect backdrop for a leisurely stroll. It was a popular excursion for Victorian folk; Baedeker's *Great Britain* notes its attractiveness for tourists. "Sightseeing is conveniently begun" near Oseney where there is Christ Church, the oldest church in Oxford, then held in great repute.

> Known among its own members as the "House" (Ædes Christi) [it] was founded by Card. Wolsey in 1525 on the site of a nunnery of the 8th cent . . . and was renewed by Henry VIII in 1546. . . . The Cathedral of the diocese of Oxford, originally the church of the priory of St. Frideswide, serves at

the same time as the chapel of Christ Church. . . . In the SE corner is the fine fan-vaulted entrance to the Hall . . . a beautiful room with a ceiling of carved oak.[38]

The "new" east window sported a stained glass by Burne-Jones, where a ship of souls carries St. Frideswide to heaven. In Haweis's mind, Chaucer's text, referencing the Abbey, the church, and Oxford's patron saint, merged harmoniously into its antiquarian environment.

Unlike "The Story of Alison" that carefully follows Chaucer's version through to the end, Haweis's subsequent essay places scant emphasis on plot, going so far as to distort it or to leave great gaps in content. For these readers, the shocking scene at the shot-window could be alleviated, alluded to, but not strictly discussed. Either the audience would have previously known what came next or Haweis surmised they would not care. When Absolon comes to the window for a kiss, for example, Alison dismisses him rudely. The essay continues:

> The second time he appears, Alison does not even take the trouble to get up. His "sweete leef" and promise of a ring do not deceive her; but hendy Nicholas, too elated to be quite as wise as usual, encounters him and his red-hot coulter so warmly that he loses his head, and his shouts for "water" at once convince the tub-hanging carpenter that Noah's flood is coming back, and put an end to his own peace as well.
>
> ("C's Char.," p. 33)

Gervase, the smith, does not figure in this parsing of the tale; there are no banging brooms; Nicholas's encounter with the coulter is left indeterminate; and Absolon's squeamishness and fastidiousness of speech remain unresolved. Haweis's magazine essay is intended for entertainment, not pedagogy. It emphasizes rural landscape, colorful clothing, working women, and illicit trysts. Still, her academic proclivities are difficult to suppress altogether, and on two occasions, she does not try. Drawing from her vast knowledge of contemporary critical issues, she argues that Chaucer's characters are not distinguished merely by costume, as had been alleged,[39] but that he "shows such a grasp of human character and so shrewd and good-humoured an insight into the intricacies of the human mind, that his figures, like those of our great Dramatist, are figures for all times" ("C's Char.," p. 26). Nor is she convinced of the poet's university education, as had been argued by Thomas B. Shaw:

> The honor of having been the place of his education has been eagerly disputed by the two great and ancient universities of Oxford and Cambridge; the former, however, of the two learned sisters having apparently the best established right to maternity – or at least the fosterage – of so illustrious a nursling. Cambridge founds her claim upon the circumstances of Chaucer's having subscribed one of his early works "Philogenet of Cambridge, clerk."[40]

For Haweis, such unsubstantiated opinions were suspect:

> Chaucer's evident familiarity with the locale of Oxford in this tale, and with that of Cambridge in *The Reeve's Tale*, no doubt originated the notion that he was educated at both universities. But this familiarity proves nothing. Chaucer is likely to have visited many a town in his capacity of royal page, valet of the Bedchamber, and King's esquire; and thus may have known Oxford by being present (possibly) at the miracle plays which took place in that city, and in which Alison's admirer Absolon figured as Herod.
>
> ("C's Char.," p. 31)

An independent and original thinker, outspoken in her views, Haweis did not hesitate to quarrel with the established male scholars of her day.

For the next several years after her article appeared in *University Magazine*, Haweis continued to write about Chaucer, but apparently, not about *The Miller's Tale*. Her textbook *Chaucer for Schools* came out in a second edition in 1881, and in 1882 her article, "More News of Geoffrey Chaucer," appeared in *Belgravia*. In 1883, however, in an article written for the *Contemporary Review*, Haweis returned briefly to the Miller's tale for an analysis of Absolon in "Colours and Cloths of the Middle Ages." Having earlier quarreled with critics who contended that Chaucer characterized by costume alone, she praises the poet and his contemporaries for realizing color in an "exact and brilliant" way, "put[ting] it before [one's] eyes as definitely as [Chaucer] saw it himself."[41] "Absolon's eyes are grey as a goose": the "soft light-grey eyes common in England, with or without blue in them, and the lashes giving a sort of furry softness to the glance."[42] He wore a

> "watchet . . . usually held to be a colour, pale blue, which is precisely the kind of colour the dandified Church Clerk would have worn with red hose."
>
> I suggest . . . that Absolon's "light watchet" was the lightest shade of a blue which is morally certain to have been sold in more than one shade: not turquoise, though described by Cotgrave as "plunket or skie-blue," but a red blue like ultramarine or cobalt, which in the darkest shade would be sapphire, or that almost violet shade still used for cassocks in great festal services in foreign cathedrals.[43]

Earlier, Tyrwhitt had defined "wachet" as a kind of cloth, "on account of some MSS. reading "whit" instead of light." But Haweis takes issue, claiming that he has misread. Ross notes that in the 1894 edition of the *Complete Works of Geoffrey Chaucer*, Skeat had "corrected" Tyrwhitt. But Haweis had corrected him first.

In 1886, the Rev. Hugh Reginald Haweis was made editor of the *Routledge World Library Series*, "a new series of the most popular and standard works in the English language."[44] The series contained thirty-six volumes, including such works as Goldsmith's plays and poems, *Gulliver's Travels*, and *Mrs. Rundell's Cookery – Sweets*. In 1887 *Tales from Chaucer* was published by Mary Eliza,

which included her prose version of *The Miller's Tale*. The Rev. Haweis's introduction to the series is particularly noteworthy for the specificity with which he
designated a particular audience: not one of children or of dilettantish females, but
one of working-class men. He writes:

> I believe that, with a wide extension of [this] franchise, the time has arrived
> for the best books to be offered to a large class hitherto almost untouched by
> such literature. . . . for the crowd of steerage passengers . . . huddled together
> hour after hour doing nothing. . . . for those thousands of bread-winners
> hurrying home nightly to growing-up families. . . . for the long, gossiping,
> yawning, gambling hours of grooms, valets, coachmen, and cabmen . . . the
> vision of "Routledge's World Library" rises before me, and I say, "This, if
> not a complete cure for indolence and vice, may at least prove a powerful
> counter-charm."[45]

Although the book's flyleaf contains enthusiastic letters to the publishers, we
seemingly cannot know if the Rev. Haweis's hope to influence such a constitu-
ency in this way was ever realized.

The original number of printed copies of *Tales from Chaucer* and their current
whereabouts is a mystery. The catalogue from the British Library indicates two
holdings of its own. OCLC WorldCat, however, lists only three world libraries as
possessing the book: copies from Cambridge, from the British Library, and from
the National Library of Scotland were "not borrowable"; the Hamilton College
Library in Clinton, New York, was willing to lend. A posting from Lynn Mayo, of
the reference department at Hamilton, however, revealed that the book had been
"missing" for several years. After a diligent search, I had been able to locate no
additional copies. On June 25, 2005, Edward Baker from Leyton, London, advertised this book through eBay. I purchased it for £17. He reported that he had found
it in a "junk shop."

The contents of this book differ from those found in Haweis's other Chaucer
texts. This one contains the "Life and Times," the *General Prologue*, and eleven
tales, not all of which were actually adapted by Haweis herself, even though she
does add the "Afterwards" ("Notes by the Way") in every case. *The Knight's Tale*
is "paraphrased" by "J. P.," as is the *Pardoner's Tale*. *The Canon's Yeoman's Tale*
and *The Squire's Tale* were paraphrased by C. Cowden Clarke. Haweis herself
paraphrased all of the *General Prologue, The Wife of Bath's Tale, The Second
Nun's Tale, The Manciple's Tale, The Doctor's Tale*, and *The Miller's Tale*.

The "Life and Times" section reflects Haweis's awareness of her new male
audience. Gone are the rhapsodies on nature, Chaucer's physical features, and
Philippa's golden hair. Instead, she describes cockfights ("there was a cockpit,
among others, at Whitehall in Chaucer's day – a sort of fourteenth-century Hurl-
ingham or "Lords")[46] and jousts (Chaucer erected the scaffold at Smithfield for
Richard II in 1390). She lists place names – Lincoln's Inn, Holborn, Millbank, and
Thames Street – familiar both to the poet and to "shop assistants" and "workers in
factories." Haweis stresses that Chaucer was a busy man, who spent much of his

time doing commissioned work. "Chaucer loved the People, wrote for the People, worked for the People,"[47] she contended. He sided with the Poor against the Rich.

That Haweis had planned from the beginning to include *The Miller's Tale* in this, her ultimate Chaucer anthology, is obvious from her introduction where she references it, remarks upon Nicholas, and curiously parallels the clerk to Chaucer himself:

> Chaucer describes both Cambridge and Oxford "scholars" in his works in a manner that implies familiarity with both places; hence the tradition that he studied at both universities, no uncommon practice. In any case, his chief studies were probably in languages and the astrolabe, like that of "hendy Nicholas" described in the "Miller's Tale;" and may we not suppose in music too, seeing how sweet a singer he became? Surely he might have said of his own undergraduate days that he – "Had learned art. . . . [and sang] so sweetly, that all the chamber rang."
>
> (p. 11)

The audience for the *Routledge World Library Series* did not require from Haweis careful scholarship on Chaucer's life. Serious critics would neither have been likely to read her text, nor to have refuted her for switching positions on Chaucer's schooling without evidence.

Knowing that she would write her closest textual rendering of *The Miller's Tale* to date, Haweis adds a caveat, which seems less likely to deter her readers than to titillate them:

> A coarse nature has a coarse tongue; and so sensitive was Chaucer lest his freer stories be cast up against him, that he *quaintly* [emphasis mine] excuses himself again and again, for touching on the rough side of nature, even in the interests of mirth. "Turn over the page and chose another tale," he says reasonably enough. Writing for the whole people, naturally no side could be left untouched; but in delicacy he compares very favorably with Dante, Boccaccio, and Shakespeare.
>
> (*Routledge*, p. 16n1)

Still, Haweis felt compelled to add in a conciliatory note that Chaucer "wrote some twenty-five *Canterbury Tales* (nineteen without a blemish, six more or less coarse), and twelve other important books, with a great number of smaller poems and songs, which have nothing coarse about them" (Routledge, p. 16 n1). Having immunized both Chaucer and herself, she prepared for her final go at *The Miller's Tale*.

In this fast-paced, prose version of the story, Haweis accentuates plot. There is no moralizing, no fashion statement, and no mention of the sights of Oseney. Alison is a "saucy girl who had not much of the matron about her." John is "old" and "so ignorant a man that he would not be advised." Nicholas was young and "silly"; Absolon "squeamish and very spiteful" (*Routledge*, pp. 54–55). The tale follows Chaucer's text carefully, but omits some rich detail: the Angelus, the chancel singing of the friars, the clerk who fell into a marle-pit. The window, however, remains intact: "under [the] bower's wall," "the shot-window which was breast-high in the wall," "the window," "opening the window." And when Absolon sprang forward for a kiss,

> the mischievous Alison rushed at him with *a broom of no great purity* [emphasis mine] which he received on his face with considerable force. Absolon, who had no patience with jokes, least of all with vulgar tricks, started back in a flame of rage.
>
> (*Routledge*, p. 62)

Unlike the innocuous implement from "The Story of Alison" that was banged into Absolon's face, this "impure broom" obviously refers to the puckish Alison's pubic hair, of which "broom" was a Victorian euphemism:

> Broom: obsolete, nineteenth-century British term for the female genital area and pubic hair, possibly based on the brush of the broom resembling pubic hair.[48]

This double entendre was at the heart of many Victorian ballads, for example, "Lish Young Buy-a Broom" and "My Man John." Absolon's fury is therefore justified.

Continuing in this sexual vein, Haweis has Absolon, "bursting with fury" and with "tow on his distaff," racing to the blacksmith and then back to the window with the hot iron blade to offer Alison a "ring."

> But his voice did not 'ring' true; moreover Alison knew him too well to think that he would forgive her first insult. . . . Nicholas [obviously naked] ran forward and hastily put up the window with a view to repeating the former successful feat. But this is always a mistake; the instant the window opened Absolon was ready with his hot coulter, and attacked him with so much vigor that whole patches of his skin flew off, so that Nicholas, much sobered, and half killed by burns and blows, shouted wildly in terrific pain (Routledge, p. 63).

John cut the rope and the neighbors laugh at his jealousy, thinking him forever "silly."

Haweis's audience for *This Miller's Tale* is canny and worldly, and her "Afterwards" indicates that she knows it. No references to puzzle jugs and innocent jokes here; no excessive moralizing. She refers instead to the ribald nature of the plot, noting (no doubt in a double sense) that it was one of those that "Chaucer excuses *quaintly*" (emphasis mine). She blames this, however, on the "uneducated" nature of the classes that spawned such actions, a category to which, assumedly, readers of the *Routledge Series* would not belong. She continues: "To those who dislike practical joking and vulgar folks, and prefer pathetic or grave stories, Chaucer says with a twinkle in his eye. . . . 'Turn over the leaf.'" She praises the story for its historical and antiquarian interests, and for its representation of the growing hostility toward Catholic clergy. Then she adds: "I have made a very slight alteration in this tale." The audience would know which one.

Mary Eliza Haweis found genius in *The Miller's Tale*. Using the original manuscripts, she made careful comparisons among them and pored over the words in the texts. She scrutinized Chaucer's rime and the meter, praising the "quaint old language" and agonizing over any simple change. She applied her considerable learning to Oxford's topography, the history of miracle plays, the fabliaux in medieval French, the origin of augrim-stones, and to a tale shunned for "indecency," "obscenity," and "grossness." She differed with Adolphus William Ward that "the less said [about the story] the better," and eagerly adapted it for all ages and social classes. In her hands it became a kaleidoscope, its pieces shifting with each new reader, each new design. Because Haweis freely cited herself in the *Routledge World Library Series*, we may assume that, at least through 1887, she had published no more on *The Miller's Tale* – and perhaps we have it all. Her papers are scattered and some of them, unlisted; boxes of miscellaneous correspondence are uncatalogued and unavailable for scholarly use. There is no systematic tabulation or her articles and speeches, or even or her art. But in this small body of work, Haweis has radically changed modern-day views of the Victorian reception of the tale. Despite the "warnings" of male scholars, it *was* read, and known, and laughed at. For Haweis, *The Miller's Tale* was "remarkable": "one of the most completely funny stories ever conceived, and written with admirable skill and comic power" (*Routledge*, p. 64).

Notes

1 Mary Eliza Haweis, "Afterwards: The Miller's Tale," ed. H. Haweis (London: George Routledge & Son): 64.
2 Mary Eliza Haweis, Columbia University Archives 23/5. Subsequent references will appear in the text, abbreviated SA ("Story of Alison") and followed by MS. numbers.
3 William Lipscomb, ed., *The Canterbury Tales of Chaucer, Completed in a Modern Version*. 3 vols. (London: J. Cooke & G . . . & J. Robinson, 1795), 1, v–xi. See also Derek Brewer, "Modernizing the Medieval: Eighteenth-Century Translations of Chaucer," in *The Middle Ages after the Middle Ages in the English-Speaking World*, eds. Marie Françoise Alamichel and Derek Brewer (Cambridge: Brewer, 1997): 103–120.
4 Dorothy Wordsworth, *Journals of Dorothy Wordsworth*, ed. E. De Sellingcourt, 2 vols. (London, 1952): 1–96 (entry for Sat., 26 Dec. 1801).
5 Charles Cowden Clarke, ed., *Tales from Chaucer Told for Young People in Which His Impurities Have Been Expunged* (1833; 2nd edn., 1870; rpt. London: Heritage Press, 1952).
6 Charles Cowden Clarke, ed., *The Riches of Chaucer* (1835; 2nd ed.; rpt. London: Heritage Press, 1870), p. 215. Clarke's statement also refers to *The Reeve's Tale* which he omits as well.
7 John Saunders, *Cabinet Pictures of English Life* (London: Charles Knight, 1841), 215. Charlotte C. Morse argues that Clarke, Saunders, and Charles Knight "were the most effective boosters of Chaucer's common readership before the university in the mid-1860's took over care and promotion of the Middle English Language and literature, including Chaucer" (Charlotte C. Morse, "Popularizing Chaucer in the Nineteenth Century," *Chaucer Review* 38 (2003): 99–125, 99).
8 Saunders, *Cabinet Pictures from of English Life*, 56. Clarke's statement also refers to *The Reeve's Tale*, which he omits as well (ibid., 215).
9 Walter W. Skeat, ed., *The Complete Works of Chaucer*, 6 vols. (Oxford, 1894), vol. 1:liii, qtd. David O. Matthews, "Speaking of Chaucer: The Poet and the Nineteenth-Century Academy," *Studies in Medievalism* 9 (1997): 5–25, 16.

10 John Urry, ed., *Works of Geoffrey Chaucer* (London: Bernard Litten, 1721), 24.

11 Velma Bourgeois Richmond, *Chaucer as Children's Literature* (Jefferson, NC: McFarland, 2005), 402–420.

12 Thomas W. Ross, Introduction to *A Variorum Edition of the Works of Geoffrey Chaucer*, Vol. II: *The Miller's Tale* (Norman: University of Oklahoma Press, 1983), 12–20. At least by the last decade of the nineteenth century, the debate about sex and literature had become heated. Critics railed at authors who felt they needed to be "realistic" in order to survive; who presented "illicit intercourse between men and women . . . in an exceptionally attractive manner"; or who had "refused to allow sex its place in creative art." See, respectively, Madame Adam, the Rev. H. Adler, Walter Besant, et al., "The Tree of Knowledge," *New Review* 10 (1894): 675–690; Thomas Bradfield, "A Dominant Note in Some Recent Fiction," *Westminster Review* 142 (1985): 537–545; D. F. Hannigan, "Sex in Fiction," *Westminster Review* 142 (1985): 616–625. See also B.A. Crakantorpe, "Sex in Modern Literature," *Nineteenth Century* 37 (1985): 607–616.

13 Some German and French authors were brave enough to tackle the work, but I have been able to locate only three articles devoted solely to it in English, although on May 24, 1849, an anonymous writer queried *Notes and Queries* about the meaning of "rubible" (MT I 3331). As recently as 1983, Ross reported that few critics have mentioned the tale by name or given it a close critical analysis. . . . When critics have not ignored the tale, they have expressed their outrage at its immorality" (Ross, *A Variorum Edition*, 13).

14 William Thoms, "Chaucer's Night Spell," *Folklore Record* 1 (1878): 145. Thoms quotes from Thomas Wright's version of CT derived from London, British Library MS Harley 7334, with which Thoms takes issue.

15 Daniel Rock, "The Paternity of Christian Doctrine – Chaucer's Night Charm," *Notes and Queries* (1850): 281.

16 Evelyn Carrington, *Folk-Lore Record* 2 (1878): 127–134.

17 Thomas Tyrwhitt, ed., *The Poetical Works of Geoffrey Chaucer* (London: 1843), 183n (Ver. 3217).

18 Anonymous, "The Song of Chaucer's Clerk of Oxenford, 'Angelus ad Virginem'," *Month* 44 (1882): 100–102, 102. Despite a rigorous search, I can find no author's name attached to this article. For a contemporary analysis of this song, see John Stevens, "Angelus ad Virginem: The History of a Medieval Song," in *Medieval Studies for J.A.W. Bennett*, ed. P. L. Heyworth (Oxford: Aetates S LXX, 1981), 297–328.

19 For less innocent speculations concerning Chaucer's choice of music, see Thomas W. Ross, "Notes on Chaucer's *Miller's Tale*, A 3216 & 3320," *English Language Notes* 13 (1976): 256–258.

20 UBC Sous Fonds, Box 23, folder 4–5.

21 I am grateful to Michael Bott, Keeper of Archives and Manuscripts at the Reading University Library, for supplying me with material from these uncatalogued records. In 2008, Siân Echard also researched some of the material in this chapter and the next in the UBC library. That same year my article "A Completely Funny Story" was published in the *Chaucer Review* 42 (2008): 244–268.

22 William Lambarde, *Dictionarium Angliae Topograph & Historicam* (Boston: Ticknor & Fields, 1730); Henry Morley, *First Sketch of English Literature in the Nineteenth Century*, 3 vols. (London: Cassel & Co., 1873).

23 Thomas E. Hill, *The Essential Handbook of Victorian Etiquette* (1873–1890); rpt. San Francisco: Bluewood Books, 1994, p. 39.

24 Robin Melrose and Diana Gardner, "The Language of Control in Victorian Children's Literature," in *Victorian Identities: Social and Cultural Formations in Nineteenth-Century Literature*, eds. Ruth Robbins and Julia Wolfrey (New York: Palgrave Macmillan, 1996), p. 69.

25 Ibid.

26 Edith Lazaros Honig, *Breaking the Angelic Image* (New York: Greenwood Press, 1988), p. 69.

27 Richmond, *Chaucer as Children's Literature*, 36.

28 Jennifer Phegley, *Educating the Proper Woman Reader* (Columbus: Ohio State University, 2004), 195.

29 Mary Eliza Haweis, "Chaucer's Characters," *University Magazine* 93:3 (1879): 30–31. Subsequent references will appear in the text with the abbreviation "C's Char."

30 Paul E. Beichner, "Characterization in *The Miller's Tale*," in *Chaucer Criticism*, I, *The Canterbury Tales: An Anthology*, eds. Richard J. Schoeck and Jerome Taylor (Notre Dame: University of Notre Dame Press, rpt. 1960), p. 124.

31 Charles Muscatine, *Chaucer and the French Tradition* (Berkeley: University of California Press, 1957), p. 230.

32 Bennett (Toronto: University of Toronto Press, 1974), pp. 55–56.

33 Ruth Cline, "Three Notes on The Miller's Tale," *Huntington Library Quarterly* 26 (Feb. 1963): 141.

34 Ibid., 135.

35 *Baedeker's Great Britain: Handbook for Travelers* (Koblance: Leipsic, 1890), 227–229.

36 Morley, *First Sketch of English Literature in the Nineteenth Century*, 100.

37 *Baedeker's Great Britain*, 229.

38 This quote is apparently from Thomas B. Shaw, "Chaucer and His Times," *Graham's American Monthly Magazine of Literature, Art, and Fashion*. Haweis does not provide a citation.

39 *Contemporary Review* 44 (1833): 423.

40 "Colours and Cloths," p. 433.

41 Ibid.

42 It is unusual for Haweis not to cite by name those scholars with whom she disagrees, but in this instance, she does not. I am unable to find earlier scholarship dealing with Chaucer's characters in this way, although it was no doubt "in the air."

43 Ross, *A Variorum Edition*, 164 n.

44 H. R. Haweis, "Routledge World Library Advertiser," in *Tales from Chaucer*, ed. William Lipscomb (London: J. Cooke, 1887), n.p. Subsequent references to Tales of Chaucer are abbreviated in the text as "T C," followed by the page numbers. The original number of printed copies of *Tales from Chaucer* and their current whereabouts is a mystery. The National Library of Scotland and the Bodleian Library contain no holdings. The catalog from the British Library indicates two holdings, but OCLC WorldCat lists only one world library as possessing the book: the Hamilton College Library in Clinton, New York.

45 H. R. Haweis, "Tales from Chaucer," n.p. (Introduction to series), in *The Canterbury Tales of Chaucer, Completed in a Modern Version*, ed. Lipscomb. 3 vols. (London: J Cooke & G. G.& J. Robinson, 1795), p. 1, pp. v–xi. See also Derek Brewer, "Modernizing the Medieval: Eighteenth-Century Translations of Chaucer," 103–120. Yale UP.

46 Jonathan Rose, *The Intellectual Life of the British Working Class* (New Haven, 2002) argues that from the 1860s to 1880s, many of the working class read (alone or in groups) those authors we now considered to be classics: Shakespeare, Dickens, Scott, and even Homer. Cheap copies were made available to them, and they recorded their experiences "in their memoirs and diaries, school records, social surveys, oral interviews, literary registers, letters to newspaper editors (published or, more revealingly, unpublished), fan mail, and even in the proceedings of the Inquisition" (ibid., 1). Richard D. Altick, *The English Common Reader: A Social History of the Mass Reading Public 1800–1900* (Chicago, 1957), also focuses on the "mass reading public in England," but his study is limited by the lack of archival sources then available.

47 "The First Draft of an Essay on Chaucer, p. 12," Sous Fonds, 23–24.

48 Although the OED does not list this usage, scatological dictionaries do. The reference is taken from http://www.sex-lexis.com (13 Nov. 2006).

4 Branching out

Reinventing Chaucer

[Those] who cannot reinvent themselves must be content with borrowed postures, secondhand ideas, fitting in instead of standing out.

Warren G. Bennes

Mary Eliza would never know it, but her work on *The Miller's Tale* had brought her tantalizingly close to what critics, both early and modern, believed to be the unattainable: uniting the scholarly and the popular Chaucer. Everyone should "know" Chaucer, it was agreed. But "know" him how? To those who labored in the archives, *knowing* him meant a close reading – microscopic, in fact – as Haweis's interpretation of the Thomas Chaucer seal indicates. Her collating of the "best" manuscripts and testing of a variety of critical readings resulted in the kind of careful, sustained analysis, mindful of connotations and nuances, that would characterize the work of the New Critics, such as I.A. Richards and William Empson. Haweis never labeled herself an "historicist," although her "Table of Historical Events" is replete with references to wars, social upheavals, and deaths of famous figures at home and abroad, all occurring within Chaucer's lifetime; her prefaces reflected the life-records she knew intimately.

Although the biography of Chaucer and the historical circumstances surrounding both the poet and his work were crucial to her, Haweis never articulated a "theory" of Chaucer criticism in our sense of the word today. Her knowledge of languages and her assertion that she was opposed to translations (even though forced by circumstances to do her own) speaks deeply to her belief that a "translation" is but another man's oblation. She believed Chaucer to have been gentle and merry and "incapable of speaking ill." Yet she was aware that secondary meanings teemed beneath his lines and that without more evidence – which might not be in the offing – we can never expect to know exactly what is there. Working closely with some of the best scholars of her time, witnessing everyday discoveries as they happened and beholding the coagulated and useless manuscripts brought over from the Record Office, Haweis knew what was and was not available as modern critics never can. She remains an anonymous keystone around which can be chiseled the "cutting-edge" scholars of today.

Haweis understood, as many members of the learned societies did not, that *any* exposure to Chaucer that she herself might orchestrate was both better than none and superior to most. She had remade Chaucer's stories for children and created a popular textbook of the *Tales*. As the remainder of this chapter will attest, she also attacked other specimens of popular culture and turned them into scholarly Chaucer teaching tools in a way that no one has ever replicated. For example, on Thursday, January 12, 1882, at her Amber House in Regent's Park, she (along with Furnivall[1]) hosted a Chaucer Ball, "the most original scheme of a costume-ball that has ever been advanced."[2] The late nineteenth century witnessed the flourishing of the costume ball. In April 1882 the *Art Amateur* printed an article on the wasteful lavishness and vanity of such parties, the ostentatious list of guests, and the extravagant dress.[3] Moreover, such occasions were replete with germs. Doctors lectured on hygiene in crowds, on the dangers of typhoid, whooping coughs, and drain fever, but to no avail; the parties carried on.

Costume parties ranged from the modest calico ball to the magnificent affairs "under the supervision of real historical artists where a curl too few or a bow too many incur the gravest censure."[4] Some costume balls required only the "dressing up" of the head, and an old gentleman stole the show by wearing "a cotton nightcap just as he would arise from the bed."[5] The author for the *Art Amateur*, one "CCH," noted that at an eclectically themed ball "last winter" (no name and no host) one man came as a "pillar letter-box" in red silk tights, a red close-fitting satin body coat embroidered with a white postage label, and a pointed head-dress, shaped like a letter. Also attending was a "hornet," in a short black satin skirt and long, pointed bodice. A framework of black and gold stripes fitted around her hips; her wings were black and green; and her black cap had the eyes and antenna of a bug. Two young ladies dressed as "dominoes," and "small twin sisters appeared as Vandyck baby maidens. Others came as white satin "Dresdin figurines," and still others were "roses" in pink and white tulle studded with petals.[6] Superficiality, decadent luxuriance, and lack of a strict thematic motif characterized such gatherings. But Haweis's ball was not like any other.

The timing for the party was propitious. *Chaucer for Children* was now in its second printing and *Chaucer for Schools* had appeared the year before. In 1879, *Dublin Literary Magazine* had published "Chaucer's Characters," and the scholarly "More News of Chaucer" was soon to come out in *Belgravia*. Never reluctant to promote herself or to instruct the public about her beloved poet, Haweis sought the aid of Arthur Lazenby Liberty (later founder of Liberty & Company) and turned her drawing room into the "Tabard Inn." In a letter to her mother dated 19/82, she wrote: "The rooms were decorated by Liberty at his own expense. I suppose he thought my name would advertise him, and his loan would have cost anyone else 8 or 10£. They were beautiful hangings."[7] The *Art Amateur* reported that "the walls were draped with soft silks of low-toned hues . . . [and] a dado [the lower portion of the wall] of cloth-of-gold with curtains and portières [heavy curtains hung across a doorway] of old Persian embroideries."[8] Candles burned in "ancient brazen candelabra, alternating with picturesque lanterns." The stage for the Tabard Inn was set.

To no one's surprise, the honored guest was Frederick Furnivall. The newspaper accounts noted that he "ordered the daunsyng," and "during the evening [the Prioress and the 'little nun'] indulged in a Highland fling, much to the amusement of the lookers-on."[9] But, like Haweis, Furnivall also understood protocol. He had completed his edition of the *Babees Book* in 1867, and it is impossible to believe that he and Mary Eliza did not insist on correct "fourteenth-century manners" from the guests:

> At the supper-time a train of Canterbury pilgrims filed into a room and took their places on one side of a long narrow trestle table, lighted with candles and served from the other side by servants in costume, reviving very successfully the picture of many an old feast seen in manuscripts of the fourteenth century.[10]

The *Babees Book* is a rich repository of table manners for children that would have delighted all of the guests: "Do not pick your nose, teeth, or nails," "do not lean on the table or dirty the cloth," or "stuff your mouth so that you can't speak," "dip your meat in the salt cellar," "put your knife in your mouth," or "cut your meat like a field laborer," its author advised."[11] Instruction on proper medieval etiquette would have been central to the preparation for this meal.

Figure 4.1 Dinner in the Olden Time
Source: *Chaucer for Children.*

Haweis herself did not write about medieval table manners, referring her audience to Furnivall's work, but in *Chaucer for Children* she included her own painting of "Dinner in the Olden Time," where

> the ordinary dinner-table or "festive *board*" in a Franklin's or burger's house . . . [were] taken from numerous fourteenth-century illustrations. . . . The carver, cupbearer, the fishbones left on the table in the absence of plates, the trenchers or slices of stale bread or buns used in lieu of them, and the other objects upon the table, are faithful copies from the MSS.

She included a minstrel playing a cittern, and behind him

> the servitors [brought] in a pasty, some small birds on spits, and the nef or ship, containing salt, liqueurs, spices, or towel, &c, for washing the hands – or, if you like, it is a *soleltè* in the form of a ship.

A subtlety, she explained, "was an ornamental dish that usually closed each course, made in some fanciful form, such as a castle, ship, or animal." The table-cloth pattern was derived from a fourteenth-century hunting horn; the floors were "strewn with sweet herbs"; and underneath the table "dogs munched on the waste victuals." With the exception of the hounds, one might assume that the setting for the Chaucer Ball would have been much like this (*CC*, p. 108).

Attire for the guests was not left to chance, as Haweis, an expert on historical costuming, deplored any mistakes in the name of Chaucer. Her diary recounts numerous visits to the British Museum to study exhibits and her commentary on these is always academic and precise. The feature in the *Art Amateur*, however, which seems partly to have been written by Haweis herself, is in a vein different from her journals as it is pitched to an audience of socialites who wanted mention of their beautifully dressed children in the press.

> What would at first sight seem too difficult, the construction of the necessary dresses, was overcome by Mrs. Haweis's very clear explanation of the main form of dress, both male and female, in the epoch indicated. For women, a close-fitting gown like that now styled the princess, the borders variously ornamented with mottoes or with garlands of embroidered flowers. For men, either a long dalmatic [wide-sleeved garment], straight, full and clinging with slits at either side to show the bright hose in walking, or a very short, close-fitting jacket, both finished with fur, jewelry, or needlework upon the borders.[12]

Mary Eliza wrote an "Afterwards" to her mother: "Our . . . fancy ball was a lot of trouble as I had to cut the dresses of the guests beside my own children [sic], the costumers knowing *nothing* about such an early period. Several papers have commented on it, of course."[13] *The Art of Beauty* (1878) contains a section on fourteenth-century dress, along with Haweis's original sketches, modeled on manuscript paintings, museum exhibitions, and a close study of the effigies at Westminster Abbey, about which she would write in her later years.[14]

Guests included the children of some well-connected London families, who provided Haweis with the extra publicity she sought. These consisted of various patrons of the pre-Raphaelites, friends of William Morris, and one Walter Crane, who had painted the elegant *Neptune's Horses*. With the exception of the "little nun" and of the Prioress, wearing a soft cashmere gown, carrying "a paire of coral beades gauded al with greene," and sporting a "broche of gold" (the Middle English suggests Haweis's own wording), the children were not dressed as pilgrims but as characters within the tales. Some of these – Arcite, Griselda, Walter, and Emelye – Haweis had already written about in articles or in "Notes by the Way." Others were new to her repertoire: Canace, from *The Squire's Tale*, carrying a magic ring and a hooded falcon; Alceste and Ariadne, in their beautiful Greek costumes of ivory silk; St. Cecilia, in her white Indian muslin "wreathed with white anemones and other real flowers." Haweis's elder son, serving as Prince Lionel of England, was accompanied by his jester, wearing a horned hat.

> A quaint and most attractive little mortal was the baby boy of Mrs. Haweis, Stephen, aged three, who appeared as the good ploughman and "trewe swynker," from the "Prologue." [Not described by Chaucer.]
> He wore a green, smock-frock, rough leggings strapped with red, black wooden shoes of the traditional shape, a hood with the inscription in Anglo-Saxon [sic] characters "God spede the plow, and sende us korne enow," and bore in his tiny hand a wooded spade of the early form.[15]

News of the party spread across the ocean. On February 19, 1882, the *Chicago Daily Tribune* reported: "Mrs. Haweis gave a Chaucer ball for children, and a supper of Canterbury pilgrims [sic], at her house in London a few weeks since. The costumes were studied from fourteenth-century manuscripts." Mary Eliza had noted to her mother "several papers picked up the party." Actually, it was bandied about everywhere.

Most of the newspaper descriptions were similar, if not identical to one another, but one from the *Nottingham Evening Post* (28 January 1882) offers a singular, significant detail. This writer had read *Chaucer for Children* and commended Haweis for her

> carefully revised edition that may be read in any nursery, *and must have been, or the tiny representatives, some not more than three years old could scarcely have acted their several parts with the efficiency that is born of understanding.*
>
> (emphasis mine)

It is here at this moment that Haweis realized – but did she know it? – all she had wanted for Chaucer: the young and the old, the popular and the academic together, in "authentic" medieval surroundings with clear evidence that the guests

knew her text and had at least a smattering of Chaucer's world, that they were act-
ing it out as she had created it for them. One would hope that she both recognized
and understood. Such a moment would not come again.

The year 1883 was a busy time for Haweis. After the ball, she published "More
News of Geoffrey Chaucer" (see Chapter 1) for the magazine *Belgravia*. Issued
in two parts, it contained a wealth of material gleaned from the Chaucer *Life-
Records*, the discoveries of her colleagues, and chiefly from her own thoughts
and reflections over the years. In addition to her account of the Chaucer seal, she
addressed the position of women during the poet's lifetime, Chaucer's influence
on the English language, his dabbling into alchemy, and his interest in Aristotelian
philosophy. With the help of newly discovered records gleaned from her archival
searches, she constructed as accurately as she could Chaucer's genealogy, his
marriage, and the lives of his children. She quoted from the deBanco rolls, from
the facsimiles of National MSS., "photo-zincographed [sic] by direction of the
Master of the rolls in 1865," and from the Parliament Act of 34 Henry VIII. Meanwhile, she cut costumes and stitched hems.

What did Mary Eliza consider the Chaucer Ball to have achieved? From those
attending, a deeper appreciation for medieval protocol and for *The Canterbury
Tales* of course. But more readers for her own works? An increase in her worth
as a scholar? All or none of the above? At stake has always been the question of
whether Chaucer can be popularized without losing those qualities that make him
a genius. Twentieth-century male scholars, confident that such could be so, have
received both praise and ire. Steve Ellis writes that

> Furnivall himself, while spearheading an enormous amount of archival and
> manuscript research aimed at establishing a reliable Chaucerian text, canon,
> and biography, had a disarmingly "unacademic" manner, announcing inter
> alia that Chaucer "ought to have been caned" for the "lame" conclusion to
> the *Book of the Duchess* and admiring his subject's eye for "all the points of
> a woman – no man knew 'em like Chaucer."[16]

To die-hard academics, Furnivall often crossed the line, a fact that might partially
explain his close friendship with Haweis, who did so as well. Ellis refers to Furnivall's introduction to Harvey Darton's *Tales of the Canterbury Pilgrims*, where
Furnivall

> *attempts*, one feels [emphasis mine], to talk to two audiences at once; the
> emphasis on Chaucer's morality is reassuring to parents, whereas children
> are told that Chaucer as a boy "was a little elvish-looking fellow . . . as bright
> and quick as a boy could be, plucky and slippy at football, hockey, and other
> games."[17]

For certain, Furnivall pitched to a double audience, but Haweis chose to do it
differently: her popular audience was expected to become scholars, and she was
willing to do the teaching it took for them to arrive at that point. Surely both

Haweis and Furnivall knew what contemporary Chaucerians now recognize as the breach between the academics and the popularizers. Still, I believe that Haweis hoped and envisioned to the end of her life that she had somehow managed to conquer this divide. As we have seen in earlier chapters, Haweis could write like a scholar, and some of her discoveries are arguably as important as those of other Chaucerians of the day. The point is, however, that other scholars did not write any other way and Haweis did. Desperate to be taken seriously, she was increasingly mindful that her female audience paid the bills, especially as her husband lavished more and more money on his mistress. Determined to make Chaucer a household name even in the most unlearned of habitats, Haweis often pleased no one for the long term, as one audience counteracted the other. Thus she occupied that precarious middle ground where even male scholars were unable or unwilling to tread: Chaucer's speech.

> The whole subject of Chaucer translation is still a contentious one, raising among other issues the fraught relationship between the more "popular" Chaucer and the Chaucer of academic study. . . . Defenders of the practice will argue for the difficulty of Middle English and the fact that the resources needed to master it are unavailable to the many even though a widespread pretense remains that modern readers can master Chaucer's language with only a "casual amount of study."[18]

Do, or *did*, translators lead readers into a deeper study of the poet in Middle English as every medievalist since Haweis has hoped? It is debatable.

Notwithstanding, brave souls have tried. Lumiansky's 1948 translation was termed "grossly misleading" and the reviewer warned that scholars were "bound to be disappointed." Howard Patch wrote that "anyone who really knows Chaucer's verse will think it perhaps better that even the beginner should be sent to the Middle English at once," and he feared that the book "might be sold to Hollywood."[19] Tom Burns Haber complained of the "omissions" and of the "unnecessary confusion [caused by] changing the generally accepted order of the tales." ("Lumiansky would have done well to bow to convention and present his tales in Skeat's order.")[20] The anonymous writer for *Time* magazine, who reviewed Nevill Coghill's "lollipop Chaucer,"[21] noted that "the rendering is literally clear and exact, but the reader who wants to feel the real teeth of an ancient winter must still turn to his unrevised Chaucer." Marvin Mudrick, however, is much more fierce:

> Mr. Coghill, like most translators, seems to believe that his performance succeeds as intact transfer: it "has a fidelity more fundamental, he says in his preface, than the surface fidelity of the crib. He is right: it makes a poor crib. Actually, when he is not mistranslating or vindictively racking the shrunken Chaucerian line or taking occasional advantage of directly useable words and rhymes, his translation is academic paraphrase, an attempt to "get at" meaning even if it means to discard images, to wreck idiom, and to caricature tone,

> in a language with no discoverable center or voice, and all of it compulsively embraced by rhyme.[22]

For Mudrick, as for most Victorian academics,

> anyone unwilling to take the trouble to use the Chaucer glossary and get up the pronunciation . . . yet willing to accept the rags and patches of Chaucer versions, is in fact doubly unfit to read Chaucer. Or, it is tempting to add, any other English poet.[23]

Chaucer, it seems, is either for the popular reader or the academic – not both. Still, it is thanks in part to Mary Eliza Haweis that Chaucer, for a very brief span of time, days, or perhaps weeks, *did* reach a double audience – when, while she discussed with scholars the rolls and records forming an account of the poet's life, she simultaneously instructed mothers on how to cut carefully prepared "medieval" patterns from brocaded white silk for their young Griseldas, to embroider Indian muslin with anemones to honor St. Cecilia, and to plait the hair of "Miss Gay" around her ears as it appeared in the statue of Edward III's daughter in Westminster Abbey.

Having reinvented the costume ball, Haweis turned her attention to another ill-conceived genre that needed her: the Victorian Birthday Book. In choosing such a genre, Haweis was either taking a deliberate chance or responding to a provocative challenge. A calendar for the year with space to write and a random-seeming verse per day appear to have been the only criteria. I can find none – not even the *Shakespeare Birthday Book* – that contains any clear sense of audience or introductory matter whatsoever. Some of these were centered on general themes – *Birthday Book of Flower and Song* or *Daily Texts and Mottoes for Young Christians*. Others, still one-dimensional in nature, focused on random quotes from a famous writer – Tennyson, Eliot, or Dickens. None could be referred to as academic or intellectual.

Yet the Victorian age witnessed the vast production of birthday books, often a source of derision by critics, who found them ubiquitous, fussy, and superficial. "To the making of birthday books there is no end!" cried one *Leeds Mercury* critic in despair.[24] The *London Daily News Critic* groused that

> The younger members of the so-called gentler sex have ever some instrument of torture. They used to keep albums. . . . This palled, as nobody wanted to read the poetry, and very few to write it. So Birthday Books are "in," and you are worried by bad pens and old blotting paper, as you write your name opposite some wholly inappropriate quotation. The more daring amateurs send their Birthday Books by post, and beseech persons whom they do not know to write in their names, stamp the wretched parcel, and return it. This is simply the most heinous form of autograph collecting, a misdemeanor, if not a felony.[25]

When George Eliot was asked to be the subject of a birthday book in 1858, she was ambivalent in the extreme. She had never heard of such and asked her publisher for advice: "Eliot feared they might be inappropriately commercial, 'the vulgarest things in the bookstalls, for what we know,' the kind of 'puffing, gaudy, clap-trappy' publication that could harm her reputation."[26] Ultimately, however, she reluctantly agreed and her publisher noted: "I have always the greatest contempt for Birthday Books . . . but George Eliot furnishes such an array of gems that one forgets the idiotic plague to which such books are turned."[27]

Determined to avoid the "idiotic plague," Haweis made *Chaucer's Beads: A Birthday Book / Diary & Concordance of Chaucer's Proverbs / or Soothsaws*, a work of literary art. Having done her homework, she avoided the mistakes of others and won the respect of a dubious public. There is evidence, albeit a bit obscure, that Furnivall helped her along the way. On November 3 (?) he had acknowledged a lost and previous communication from Haweis:

> I'm very glad to hear of Chatto's proposal and I'm certain that you can do the book and do it well. The plan of it you must settle yourself. . . . I should think that the index would serve as a Glossary. Any help I can give you, I will gladly.[28]

The book under discussion seems to have been announced by the *Literary World* on August 11, 1883, Haweis's original binding was in black and red print, which "was suggested by the colours of Chaucer's own beads – black with a red string – which he is represented as carrying, in the two only authentic portraits of him in the British Museum"[29] – although it was published not by Chatto & Windus, but by W. H. Allen & Co.,[30] who had that same year published Hugh Haweis's *My Musical Life*.[31] Within its genre, Mary Eliza's work is a tour de force. On July 19, 1884, the *Graphic* stated:

> "Chaucer's Beads" is the somewhat fanciful title of a handsome birthday book compiled from the works of the father of English poetry by Mrs. Haweis. . . . We do not agree with all the author's comments, but on the whole the work is well and carefully done. One unidentified critic from the *Daily News* wrote that "Chaucer's Beads" . . . aims at providing a birthday book, a diary, and a concordance of Chaucer's proverbs all in one. It is pretty to the eye, with its rubric letters, limes, and other ornaments."

He added, however, a caveat: "We can only hope that it does not give the folk who delight in birthday books *more credit than they deserve* for curiosity regarding old literature and proverbial wisdom" [emphasis mine].[32] In other words, by mere purchase price one did not become an intellectual, even though Haweis, who put much time and effort into this work, clearly hoped some of them might. The archives of Haweis's publisher, W. H. Allen, are no longer extant and there is no evidence regarding the number of copies sold. If Haweis were successful in luring the pedestrian reader to be scholarly, we cannot know whether she accomplished it.

In her "Foreward," Haweis, tongue-in-cheek, not only deprecates the entire category of birthday books, which she must have found abhorrent, but she also teasingly undercuts her own work: "Birthday Books are so fashionable that there is plenty of room for a new Birthday Book," she iterates.[33] *Her* version, however, reflecting erudition, close reading, and the summoning of relevant scholars and texts, is worthy of careful observation. In the nineteenth century, Chaucer scholars did not write about Chaucer's proverbs, so Haweis could not turn to previous works as models.[34] This absence of such scholarship perplexed her, for she argued that Chaucer's proverbs "had a broad class appeal and [could] profitably be studied to learn more about 'Old English'" (the nineteenth-century term for "Middle English"). She turned to a book by Ulick Ralph Burke on *Sancho Panza's Proverbs*, published in 1877,[35] for a model. Burke was not a scholar per se. He begins with a rambling introduction of sorts, praising Spanish proverbs, especially Castilian ones, and defining them as "short sentences drawn from long experience." He traces the origins of such sayings, noting that in Spain "proverbs are in everyone's mouth, high and low; and have a national aroma very interesting historically." He wonders why they were not popular in England.[36] To Haweis, they clearly should have been. Her introduction reveals that she pondered over the meanings of Chaucer's words and expressions and sought origins in other languages. Puzzling over the Pardoner's use of "blakeberied" in that pilgrim's comments about his "clients" – "I never cared, when they are once buried, their souls may go blackberrying – "[37] she seeks equivalents in both French and Polish maxims, before concluding that "plenty as blackberries" was a common saying. "To go blackberrying would take long, and lead [the souls] far." *The Riverside Chaucer* glosses "blakeberied" simply as "play truant,"[38] thus omitting, as a modern annotator would ordinarily do, the thought processes that led to the final gloss. In addition to tracing her own musings, Haweis reveals a close reading of the text itself regarding this particular proverb, pointing to the repetition of the couplet rimes "beried" and "blake*beried*" at the ends of 11.405–406. "It always seems to me not an accident nor want of skill in a rhymester so accomplished as Chaucer," she observes, "to reproduce words in such close succession. It is more likely to be an intentional play on the word," though she confesses she does not know exactly what that play would be. As a seeming afterthought, she adds, "It would be interesting to collect Chaucer's puns."

Haweis's easy acceptance of Chaucer's use of puns was exceptional in 1884, when it was generally considered that the poet avoided this low form of wit.[39] It was not until eight years later, in fact, that Thomas Lounsbury reluctantly suggested that the poet had used a *single* pun: a play on the word "style" in *The Squire's Tale* ("Al be it that I kan nat sowne his stile"). "Still, from conceits of all kinds and of all grades Chaucer's language, at every period of his literary career, was in general wholly free,"[40] Lounsbury proclaimed. Haweis clearly did not agree.

On October 16, 1883, Haweis received one letter from Furnivall and another on what appears to be November 3 of the same year (UBC, Box 3–9). He writes,

> Why [don't ??] you leave out your *Canterbury* article for me? Then I could read it and return it soon.
>
> Always devotedly yours.
F.J.F.

It is unclear what "*Canterbury* article" Furnivall refers to here. Haweis's first Chaucer article was "Chaucer's Characters," published in 1879. "More News of Geoffrey Chaucer" had been out for a year, and there was not another article on the horizon. Her essay on "Colours and Cloths of the Middle Ages," which *was* published in 1883, is by no stretch of the imagination a "*Canterbury* article." Furnivall can only have been referring to *Chaucer's Beads*.

Was Lounsbury ignorant of Haweis's book? Who was the audience for *Chaucer's Beads*? Except for a single curious mention in 1934 one might assume that the "small popular book" crumbled into dust in Victorian attics among pressed flowers and dress-up dolls. However, when reviewing another book of maxims, Bartlett Jere Whitings' *Chaucer's Use of Proverbs* (1934), scholar Margaret Galway compared that work to Haweis's, and compared it *un*favorably. She states: "had Dr. Whiting followed the example of two earlier collectors of Chaucer's proverbs, Skeat and *Mrs. Haweis* [emphasis mine], in supplying a finding-index [i.e., Furnivall's proposed index], the value of his work to scholars would have been greatly enhanced."[41] Skeat's book, *Early English Proverbs* was not published until 1910,[42] twenty-six years after *Chaucer's Beads*. Haweis's work, then, is the first issued scholarship on Chaucer's proverbs.

Searching carefully through the then-known corpus of Chaucer's works,[43] she selected 365 phrases and formulated a methodology of her own. The months of January, February, and March were devoted to the *Troilus and Criseyde*, which Haweis considered to have been an "early work." These were followed by lines from the minor poems, with the bulk of the remaining text belonging to *The Canterbury Tales*. She ended with an appendix of other proverbial phrases in Chaucer. Then she appended, not a glossary, but "An Alphabetical Table Containing All the Principal Saws [mottoes] Quoted in This Book" – the finding-index that Furnivall would subsequently suggest and that Galway would admire.

Bartlett Jere Whiting was either unaware of *Chaucer's Beads* or choose to ignore it. "The first collection of Chaucer's proverbs *of any scope*," he announced (emphasis mine), "was made by Willi Haeckel (1890), but it is without introductory comment on Chaucer's usage, and is incomplete."[44] Klaeber's *Das Bild bei Chaucer* (1893) is "over-arranged," not "useful" for reference; Skeat's *Early English Proverbs* (1910) is large of bulk but not developed; and Skeat "was not especially interested in proverbs" anyway, Whiting noted.[45] But Mary Eliza Haweis's collection of sayings predated all of the above. Written, apparently, by the first Chaucerian to have judged Chaucer's soothsaws as worthy of isolation and study and who freely acknowledged Chaucer's puns. In the introduction to *The Concordance to the Complete Works of Geoffrey Chaucer*, Tatlock, himself a recognized literati, divided his Concordance "helpers" into two distinct categories: "those who had been or became persons of distinction in scholarship" and "others." "Mrs. Haweis," who wrote "peppery letters" and who "had done much to *popularize* Chaucer" (emphasis mine), is manifestly an "other."[46]

Much time and effort went into the making of *Chaucer's Beads*, but the original audience for whom it was intended is a conundrum. Clearly, it is pitched to scholars, to linguists, and to those who had an in-depth knowledge of the poet and of the languages he spoke and read. She calls it a "small, popular book, and apologizes to 'scholars' for changing the spelling to avoid stumbling blocks for the readers"(p. ix). Her entry for March 8 is but one example taken from *The Legend of Good Women*:

> For whoso geveth a gefte or doth a grace
> Do it betime, his thank shal be the more.
> (*Prologue*, l. 451)

> Lit. – *Who gives a gift or does a kindness, let him do it betimes, he will be more thanked.*
>> French equiv, – "*Qui donne tôt, donne deux fois.*"
>> Spanish equiv. – "*El que luego da, da dos vecces.*"
>> Latin equiv. – "*Bis dat cito dat.*"
>> Given quickly is twice given.

For this quotation, Haweis translates in French, Spanish, and Latin, but for other entries she quotes from Scots, Old Spanish, Hebrew, and Old Italian. Her diaries indicate her fluency in French and she might have been studying Arabic, but so many languages seem excessive. Who was her intended reader? The acknowledged audience for birthday books was women, and uneducated women at that! Unlike her other scholarly works, this one has no mention of Furnivall or the Chaucer Society, or anyone who had mentored her – although apparently Furnivall did.

One is apt to find literary gems in Haweis's works, sometimes buried down deep in her notes, and *Chaucer's Beads* does not disappoint. Modern scholars still puzzle about the "Kynges Note," sung by Nicholas in *The Miller's Tale*. In 1829, 1894, and 1928, respectively, Joseph Ritson, Skeat, and Manly speculated that "Chaucer was referring to a song mentioned in *The Complaint of Scotland . . ., King Villyamis Note.*"[47] Manly proposed that the song might even have been ribald, although Collins disagreed, citing the following line "Ful often blessed was [Nicholas's] mery throte." For Collins, the tune was probably a "sequence," beginning *Ave rex gentis Anglorum*, popular in the fourteenth century and adapted to refer to any king who was also a saint; hence, St. Edmund.[48] Frost suggested that the song was Scottish and that it was music that Chaucer referred to, rather than the words. The nationality did not concern Frost, although he admitted that the work was not printed until 120 years after Chaucer had used it.

Haweis weighed in as well. For her, the "Kynges Note" was a *chant royal*, "the name of a certain sort of poetry in which the rimes of a rather complex stanza were repeated continually. Probably all of Chaucer's ballades in which the verses rime with one another, are instances of the *chant royal*" (p. 110). She cites "Empty Purse" and "Gentilesse" as other examples of the genre. The "Kynges Note" is still unidentified, but those who wrestle with its identity cite Ritson, Skeat, Manly, Collins, and Frost. Haweis's theories lie buried among the pages of her extraordinary little book.

The same year that *Chaucer's Beads* appeared, Mr. Henry Arthur Jones produced a "Chaucerian play" at Haymarket that was universally panned. Written in blank verse which alternated between "graceful and flowing" and "ragged and labored," it "brought Chaucer to the nineteenth century rather than the reverse."[49] The fourth annual Arts & Crafts exhibition in New Gallery displayed a "table centre" by Alice Russell, "representing a border of daisies with lines from Chaucer."[50] And the *Glasgow Herald* (January 22, iss. 19) published a "negative by comparison" review of Haweis's *Chaucer for Children* book with *Chaucer's Stories* by Mary Seymour. The critic admitted that Mary Eliza had set a "good example" for Miss Seymour but rejoiced that at last "a plain version of some of [Chaucer's] stories" had appeared that would surely implant in children's minds "a delight and respect for the poet as well as lead them in riper years to study his pages with intellectual delight." Two years later, Rev. and Mrs. Haweis visited New York and she was told to her great pleasure that *Chaucer for Schools* was used "largely" in American schools. *Chaucer for Children* was reissued in 1886, and reviews of that book, as well as those of *Chaucer for Schools*, began to appear again with regularity.

In 1887, Haweis published *Tales from Chaucer* (see Chapter 3), which would have taken considerable time and effort, for this intended audience would be different from all the others. The text would be in modern English, a fact that must have galled her, and instead of targeting children or women she focused on *men* who needed some fruitful way to spend their idle time. Haweis translated the *General Prologue* and five of the tales herself (*The Miller's*, *The Wife of Bath's*, *The Second Nun's*, *The Manciple's*, and *The Doctor's*), and did passably well. Take, for example, the Manciple, whose description is murky at best:

> There was a decent Manciple of a college – so canny in his victualing business that by any system, credit or cash payment, he could feather his nest. Now is not this a providential grace, that such a common fellow's brains should outwit the wisdom of a heap of learned men? Thrice ten masters had he had, none of them fools – in his house there were a dozen fit to manage the property of any lord in England and teach him to live comfortably out of debt on his own income (unless he was mad) or to live close if he liked, and help a whole shire if necessary – and of all these masters, the Manciple outwitted every one.
>
> (p. 26)

Other tales Haweis farmed out: *The Canon's Yeoman's Tale* and that of the Squire were done by Cowden Clarke; *The Prioress's Tale* by Wordsworth; and *The Knight's* and *The Pardoner's* by an unidentified "J.P." The titles "Notes by the Way," changed to "Afterwards," were all written by Haweis, and these are more daring and capricious in *Tales from Chaucer* than in those from her other works. The *Routledge Series* would not appeal to scholars, and the working men of London would be unlikely to quibble at her premises. She includes no acknowledgments, no footnotes, no references to the Chaucer Society. Her commentaries have been carefully edited from *Chaucer for Schools*. References to other critics, to Marenduzzo's *Cento Novelle Antiche*, to living personages, and to alternative interpretations of passages have been carefully excised.

That same year she published in *Belgravia* "Words, from the Underworld," a series of melodramatic sketches mostly about animals, and began work on the "Chaucer Calendar for 1887, with Optional Motto for Leapyear," which she would not complete. The "Calendar," housed in the archives of the Columbia University Library, is a long and languid work, devoid of energy and lacking in any editorial matter from the author. It contained an "optional motto" for every day of the year, selected seemingly at random, glossing difficult Middle English words. Unlike Haweis's preceding publications, there is no notice in contemporary newspapers or magazines that this work was to be expected. That year Mary Eliza had complained of not feeling well, of being "ill again," and of "becoming antiquated."[50] Her husband was doling out to blackmailers and creditors, still spending at an alarming speed, and she could not seem to work hard enough to keep up with all the bills. The spiritless work on the calendar reflects such weariness. Still, she managed to write "Jewels and Dress: Of the Philosophy of Jewels" for *Contemporary Review*[51] and "The Art of Christmas Decorations" for *The Magazine of Art*.[52] The former is a throwback to *The Art of Beauty*, while the latter argues that religious motifs from medieval cathedrals and the Catacombs might appropriately be used at the holiday season.

While we can assume that most – if not all – of Haweis's articles are extant, the same is not true for the many speeches and lectures delivered throughout her life. In 1890, fifteen years after *Chaucer for Children* and nine years after the first publication of *Chaucer for Schools*, a reviewer for the *Bristol Mercury and Daily Post*[53] wrote:

> A week ago I had the pleasure of hearing a lecturette, given by Mrs. Haweis, the wife of the well-known preacher, in her own pretty drawingroom in the Queen's House, Cheyne walk, Chelsea, on her New Chaucer theory, and no one could have interested me more, for her version of "Chaucer for children" is in itself delightful, and is largely used in the schools of America. . . . Such a pleasant half hour we spent listening to Mrs. Haweis's discourse on her favorite poet adds much to the interest of her afternoon "At Homes," of which she has lately given eight. . . . On the Chaucer afternoon, I saw Dr. Furnivall listening with interest to what Mrs. Haweis had to say . . . and [she] spoke gratefully of the assistance he had kindly given to her in her researches.

By sheer luck, this particular at-home speech, and this one only, can be precisely identified.

Despite being touted as a "new theory" of Chaucer, Haweis's speech contains little that she had not written about throughout much of her life. We can never reconstruct her audience for the occasion, but it was likely to have been upper-middle-class individuals (mostly women) who were fairly well read. Furnivall may have been the only *literary* scholar present, and he already knew what she would say. After a nod to the Chaucer Society for publicizing the poet and a retelling of the conversion of Richard Green, she turned to Chaucer's "unique & historical position." She compared him favorably to Shakespeare (who inherited a language "ready made") and to his own contemporaries – Langland, Wiclyff, Gower, and Strode, whose language lacked his plasticity and song. She talked about Chaucer's patron, John of Gaunt, Edward III, the Church, and the balancing act of playing the game. In Chaucer's time "it was difficult enough to say anything at all, & how to say it well was infinitely more so [sic]" (p. 8). Chaucer hid his "liberty of thought" well beneath his lines, and she quotes from *The Knight's Tale*: "Great was th'effect, and high was his entent: / Well wist he why, and what, thereof he meant."

Chaucer knew what he was "about," even if others didn't, and the result of his "deviant ways" (Haweis does not elaborate) was a richer and more momentous life.

> William of Wykiham was banished & impoverished: & though he was afterwards restored, it was only after immense losses & indignities. Wiclif was practically crushed. Langland was kept obscure by his poverty, and if he fostered the hostility of the commons against the upper classes, he never got the ear of those about the Crown who might have done something to ameliorate the people's hard lot. Bishop Sudbury was butchered. But Geoffrey Chaucer – Poet, courier, Philosopher, democrat who delivered [???] as resolutely as Sudbury of Wiclif – kept to the end, through the bounty of the Crown, the means & the leisure to prosecute studies which did more good to Freedom than any premature & futile Revolution: and after vibrating with the wisest leaning towards Order; & the healthiest & sanest popular sympathies, between the Poles of conservation & Radical politics, Geoffrey Chaucer at last
> Died in his Bed!

So ends the speech, which is filled with references to male scholars, not only Furnivall and Green, but also Professor Childs of Harvard; Professor Skeat (who was finally "coming around" to her way of thinking); and Professor Hales of Queen's College, who delivered eloquent lectures on *The Canterbury Tales*. Thus, Haweis established her "credentials," and she noted that "Chaucer is also a main feature in the Home Reading Union Scheme which has branches throughout England" (p. 6).

Attached precariously to the speech manuscript is a small but important scrap of paper, which reads:

> I should have liked to read a little of Troilus to show how finished his versification is – such as the love letter of Troilus to Cressida – but it is rather long, so my daughter will recite a short bit from the N.P.Tale as a specimen of Chaucer in his more playful mood.

> (n.p.)

In the review of the speech for the *Bristol Mercury*, the reporter remarked,

> A young daughter of Mrs. Haweis's gave us on this occasion a charming little recitation from these stories [*The Canterbury Tales*], "The Priest's Tale," a legend of the cock and the fox, in the original dialect.

The two pieces match precisely.

To concentrate so intently on Mary Eliza's innovations and close readings of Chaucer's words is to forget that she was also an artist who had travelled widely and wrote about those riches she saw always with Chaucer in mind. Opening herself to a different, artistic audience, she likened the poet's methods to such painters as Donatello, Fra Angelico da Fiesole, Agnolo Gaddi, and Jan Van Eyck, and she adapted a portrait of the poet for the frontispiece of *Chaucer for Schools* ("from the drawing by Occleve"). As a painter of pilgrim portraits herself, Haweis was naturally curious about Chaucer's own physical appearance and she was not willing to accept standard lore without investigation. The frontispiece to *Chaucer for Children* contained a portrait she herself had adapted, based on an anonymous work from the National Portrait Gallery (NPG 532) and she refers to two of his three manuscript portraits (Harleian MKS 4866 and BL MS Royal 17 D. vi. F93v) housed in the British Museum, which she erroneously believed to have been painted by Hoccleve. More interesting to her, however, was the *missing* portrait of Chaucer: "probably the best, a full-length, [which] was ruthlessly cut out before Elizabeth's reign." "Who was this mischievous Antiquary?" she wondered. Haweis had personally examined the manuscript and pondered the cut-out portrait. She noted that next to the aperture was a poem composed in "rude doggerel":

Off worthy Chawcer	Summe furious foole
Here the pickture stood,	Have cutte the same in twayne;
That much did wright,	His deed doe shewe
And alle to doe us good;	He bare a barren brayne.

Haweis believed that it had been written sometime during the reign of Queen Elizabeth.[54]

In searching for material on this missing portrait, I can find no critic other than Haweis who attempted to solve its mystery or speculated on the cause of the theft or the fate of the painting. For Haweis, these likely involved Nicholas Brigham himself, who erected the poet's monument in Westminster Abbey in 1556 and who

> caused to be carven on Chaucer's tomb a *full-length portrait of the poet*: [since vanished] and who could scarce have got a stone-cutter to carve such an effigy without some picture to copy. He may have meant to slip it back, but the loss was discovered, or the scrap of vellum gut destroyed in the workshop, and he had to comfort himself that, similar to him who rebuilt Rome, he found the portrait of parchment and left it in marble.

The effigy on the tomb has crumbled away, and quite disappeared. Would that somebody could ferret out the descendants of Brigham, trace out his habits and the dispersal of his goods, and we might prove that his pretty compliment to Chaucer in the grave-place of his child sprang from intelligent interest in *all* his relics, by the recovery of *some*.[55]

No one has explored this further, and we still do not know where the missing portrait has gone. But on July 20, the same year the article appeared in London, the *New York Times* published Haweis's entire Brigham section with no comment and no attribution. In his 1900 lecture on "The Portraits of Geoffrey Chaucer," Marion Harry Spielmann, English author and art critic, suggested simply that Brigham's wall painting had been "copied from some unknown miniature." He does not say which one.[56]

Haweis was always fascinated by Chaucer and art, whether it be his portrait paintings done by others or the likenesses he created in his works, and she compared him to the Italian sculptors – Brunelleschi, Donatello, Ghiberti, and Fra Angelico (like Gothic artists, "[Chaucer] will go all round a subject . . . and present it from every point of view.") – and to Netherlandish painters, whom she believed to have been more contemporary with the poet than they actually were. Like Jan van Eyck, for example, "Chaucer created pictures teeming with rich detail, [where] everything ha[d] a meaning and a purpose."[57] Like David Teniers the Younger, "he produced [interactive] crowd scenes, rich conglomerates of peasant life, of nuns, burghers, and knights, and he always worked with a human, often humorous, touch." Like Gerhard Douw,[58] Chaucer's canvas was smooth and meticulously detailed, and he framed his personages within niches and borders.[59] Haweis's ability to close-read a painting added immeasurably to her understanding of Chaucer's texts and gave her a dimension that her contemporaries were denied.

Were her comparisons commonplace? In 1906 Robert K. Root would write that the widow's farm and the hue and cry from *The Nun's Priest's Tale* "have all the vividness and realism of a Dutch genre painting by *Teniers* or *Gerard*" (emphasis mine).[60] One hundred years later, Derek Brewer noted that

> Chaucer's density of detail in town and domestic life is quite unparalleled . . . in medieval literature. . . . And indeed, wherever one looks the eye can follow out material reality continuously to a seeming depth of perspective, *like a fifteenth-century Flemish painting*.
>
> (emphasis mine)[61]

Had Haweis been of another age, she might have evoked Erwin Panofsky's theories of "hidden symbolism," for she knew that Chaucer could "sketch" but he could also "veil," and that his characters

> are no longer conceived as relief forms integrated with and esthetically predicated upon the walls, piers, or webs to which they are attached; they have

been crystallized instead into . . . *colonettes* and *nervures*, independent tubular forms which contrast with the walls piers and webs as plastic entities having an axis within themselves. . . . Moving and turning, they seem to have emancipated themselves from the pictorial surface, and plastic values are no longer suggested by flat strips and patches of color but stimulated by a continuous modeling.[62]

Or as Haweis put it, Chaucer creates his characters "and he turns [them] inside out relentlessly. He very seldom analyses thought or motive, but he shows you what *is* so clearly, that you know what *must* be without his telling you" (*CS*, p. 49). (In another context she adds, "All his touches have a meaning and a purpose.")[63]

"More News of Geoffrey Chaucer" ends with a plea that Chaucer be read in an interdisciplinary sense, for his "general culture: history, philology, and many things besides versemaking." Haweis commended in writing the Royal Military Academy, Woolwich, which always required its students to read and study Chaucer. By the time of her essay, candidates for commissions in the regular army were required to have a knowledge of the *General Prologue* and sometimes of *The Knight's Tale* as well, along with works by Spencer, Shakespeare, Milton, and Bacon. The directive had its detractors, who argued that such materials were irrelevant to the careers of soldiers who would have been better served by studying the history of wars or the lives of the great commanders. But the opponents felt that the study of gentility and courtliness should accompany that of the arts of war.

The issue was controversial enough to have been the subject of several parliamentary debates. For example, on Friday, July 24, 1875, in the House of Lords, Lord Harrowby, citing a preference for Froissant's *Chronicles* over Chaucer's poetry, questioned the usefulness of a competitive examination on *The Canterbury Tales* as a prerequisite to the military service.[64] Such material would, he insisted, "bring the whole subject of military education into contempt." Lord Cardwell replied that

> the object of the examinations was to ascertain that the candidate desirous of entering the army had the education of an English gentleman and the military education would commence afterwards. If the education of the English gentleman had no reference to Chaucer, he should think it a very imperfect one.

Lord Cardwell was supported by Lord Stathnairn, who then read aloud a few passages from the *Tales* that he considered to be "simply abominable," but the reporter wrote that "his Lordship's literary criticism could scarce be said to be very deep or very broad." Until the end of her life, Haweis campaigned for Chaucer to be universally read by anyone attempting to lay the foundations of a liberal education. When Parliament adjourned, the motion to modify the examinations was out; Chaucer was in.

On August 11, 1883, when the *Literary World* announced that Mrs. Haweis was compiling a "Chaucer Birthday Book," she wrote a series of sketches that were never published: "Old Boys: London in the Middle Ages," "Old Boys: The

Country in the Middle Ages," and "Old Boys (Tudor Times)," now housed in the archives of the University of British Columbia Library. Although these pieces were "completed" in that they come to an end, none was actually "finished," as they show numerous signs of Haweis's editing. Never able to put aside Chaucer for long, she referred in these sketches to *The Miller's Tale* with the Cleric who "played Herod on a stage high." She also mentions "tilting at quinten," the tilting at "fan" referred to in *The Cook's Prologue* as a game played by city boys, and she sketched the machine used for such a sport, adding that a peacock was often given as a prize.

Lest it seem that the literary career of Mary Eliza Haweis started off strongly focused and ended with an anemic group of purposeless sketches, that is not the case. In the BBC archives is a letter by Haweis written on November 11, 1897, to her son Lionel: "Did I tell you that I have charge of the Chaucer course in the 'National Home Reading Union'?" she asked. That revelation, a chance sentence tucked away in an archive, is the subject of this final chapter.

Notes

1 A writer for *The Era* on Saturday, 21 January 1882 referred to Furnivall as "Furnivall the Chaucer scholar." Clearly, to this writer, Haweis did not fit into the "scholarly" category.
2 *Birmingham Daily Post*, 17 Jan. 1882: iss. 7353.
3 CCH, "Notes on Dress," in *The Art Amateur: A Monthly Journal Devoted to Art in the Household (1879–1903)* (Apr. 1882); 6, 5, 108. On Friday, 17 January 1882, iss. 7353, the *Birmingham Daily Post* published an article under "London Gossip" arguing that such balls were "hateful institutions." "A new device for expense on the part of the parents" and for "exciting envy and hatred in the bosoms of the children." The writer refers especially to Children's Balls, Calico Balls, and the Shakespeare Ball (which no other newspaper seems to have picked up).
4 *Graphic*, 3 Apr. 1880.
5 "The Ladies Column," *Manchester Times*, 27 Jan. 1877.
6 *Birmingham Daily Post*, 17 Jan. 1882.
7 Haweis clipping UBC, Box 31–3 n.d., no citation.
8 CCH, "Notes on Dress," 109.
9 Ibid.
10 Ibid.
11 *EETS*, N. Trübner, 1868, pp. 27, 80, 10, 7, 78, 20.
12 CCH, "Notes on Dress."
13 "Letter to Her Mother," UBC Sous Fonds, 22–25.
14 Candace Barrington, in "'Forget What You Have Learned'; The Mistick Krewe's 1914 Mardi Gras Chaucer," *American Literary History* 22:4 (2010), describes a Mardi Gras procession entitled "Tales from Chaucer," which consisted of twenty "static tableau mov[ing] through the streets on mule-drawn wagons, flanked by black men carrying flambeaux. . . . each fantastically-decorated float depicted an exemplary narrative moment from [various] Chaucerian works" (ibid., 807). Although the float "targeted various audiences with different messages," "distorting the medieval author beyond recognition. . . . Nevertheless, it allow[ed] American culture to engage with Chaucer, ensuring that the medieval poet continue[d] to retain canonical status as he circulates in our poet-medieval culture" (ibid., 809).
15 CCH, "Notes on Dress."

16 Steve Ellis, *Chaucer at Large* (Minneapolis: University of Minnesota Press, 2001), 18, remarks that "Furnivall's editions and notes were directed toward as wide and inclusive an audience as possible." Stephanie Trigg (*Congenial Souls*, Minneapolis: University of Minnesota Press, 2002), contends that "for the first time if only temporarily scholarly Chaucer studies took for granted an extensive public sphere" (p. 165). However, in the field of Chaucer studies Furnivall is regarded with ambivalence: sometimes as a father figure to be embraced, sometimes as an embarrassing enthusiast; and more recently as a proponent of middle-class British imperialism or rampant homosociality (ibid. 166). David Matthews (*The Making of Middle English, 1765–1910*, Minneapolis: University of Minnesota Press, 1999, 160–161, 172) argued that "while Furnivall was instrumental in creating Middle English as an academic subject of study, in part through the publications of the EETS and in part through integrating the study of Chaucer with Middle English, he also unwillingly oversaw the displacement of interest away from private individuals into university institutions" (quoted by Trigg, *Congenial Souls*, 263n).

17 Ellis, *Chaucer at Large*, 50.

18 Ibid., 98.

19 Rev. Howard Patch, "*The Canterbury Tales* of Geoffrey Chaucer," *Modern Language Notes* 64:7 (1949): 500–501.

20 Rev. John Haber, "*The Canterbury Tales* of Geoffrey," *College English* 11:1 (1949): 53–54.

21 *Time Magazine*, 11 Aug. 1952, http://time/magazine/article/0.9171.857353–2.00.html, n.p.

22 Mudrick, *The Hudson Review*, 6:1 (1953): 129.

23 Ibid. See also Ellis, *Chaucer at Large*, 98–120.

24 *Leeds Mercury*, 23 July 1883: iss. 14130.

25 *London Daily News*, 11 Jan. 1890: 5.

26 As cited by Maura Ives, " 'The Summit of the Author's Fame': Victorian Women Writers and the Birthday Book," in *Women Writers and the Artifacts of Celebrity in the Long Nineteenth Century*, eds. Ann R. Hawkins and Maura Ives (Burlington: Ashgate, 2012), 104.

27 Ibid., 105.

28. UBC, 3–9; F-20.

29 *Chaucer's Beads, Folcroft Library Editions*, 1973 (rpt. 1884), xi.

30 Little of Chatto's correspondence for Haweis is extant, but what exists refers to making – or not making – a profit on her *Chaucer for Schools*. Furnivall's advice that "Chatto should pay you a royalty on every copy sold" (F-21) might have altered any prior plans the press had made.

31 Due to the unprocessed state of the Haweis archives and of much of the Furnivall material, it is difficult to establish the extent of the communication between these individuals; the contents of the two extant letters from the University of British Columbia's Haweis Family Fonds, however, clearly indicate that somewhere more letters await discovery. These are written in Furnivall's eccentric handwriting, but the date "1883" is, in both cases, typed onto the top of the letter sheet. This may have been done later on by Stephen Haweis who donated most of the papers to UBC and periodically supplied dates from his own memory. At any rate, the 1883 date is consistent neither with the activities alluded to by Furnivall, nor with Haweis's publication record.

32 *Graphic*, 28 Nov. 1884.

33 *Chaucer's Beads*, 5. See also the self-effacing rationale of *Chaucer for Children* ("Chiefly for the use and pleasure of my little Lionel," n.p.) and *Chaucer for Schools* ("Even very young children are capable of understanding and enjoying [Chaucer's] poems when placed before them in a pleasant form," xi).

34 In 1879, F. G. Fleay listed some of Chaucer's "proverbs" in an attempt to differentiate his "pithy sayings" from "genuine folk words," but he does not discuss them further. "Some Folklore of Chaucer," *Folk-lore Record* 2 (1879): 136–142.

35 Ulick Ralph Burke, *Sancho Panza's Proverbs & Others Which Occur in Don Quixote* (London: Pickering & Chatto, 2nd ed. 1877).

36 Ibid., xix.

37 *Chaucer's Beads*, 6.

38 *The Riverside Chaucer*, ed. Larry D. Benson (Boston: Houghton Mifflin, 1987), 907n406.

39 For a later assessment, see Paul Baum, "Chaucer's Puns," *PMLA* 71:1 (Mar. 1956): 225–246.

40 Thomas Loundsbury, *Studies in Chaucer* (New York: 1892), III, 319. Even in 1916, Tatlock admits to very few puns on the poet's part. See "Puns in Chaucer," in *Flugel Memorial Volume* (Stanford, CA: Stanford University, 1916), 228–232.

41 Rev. Barlett Jere Whiting, *Chaucer's Use of Proverbs* (Cambridge: Harvard University Press, 1934), in *Modern Language Notes* 50 (1935): 334–335. In "Chaucer's Puns," Paul Baum credited Tatlock for having first noticed Chaucer's puns in 1916. He then moves on to Helge Kökeritz's article on "Rhetorical Word Play," written in 1954.

42 Walter W. Skeat, *Early English Proverbs: Chiefly of the Thirteenth and Fourteenth Centuries, with Illustrative Quotations* (Oxford: Clarendon Press, 1910).

43 She also included "The Cuckoo and the Nightingale," which the nineteenth century thought Chaucer had written, and the *Romance of the Rose*, considered "doubtful."

44 Whiting refers to *Willibald Hæckel's Das Sprichwort bei Chaucer*, published in 1890 for Vol. 8, *Erlanger Bertrage zur Englischen Philologie.*

45 Whiting, *Chaucer's Use of Proverbs*, 6.

46 John S. Tatlock, "Introduction," in *A Concordance to the Complete Works of Geoffrey Chaucer* (Gloucester, MA: Peter Smith, 1963; rpt. 1927), xi.

47 Fletcher Collins, "*The Miller's Tale*, Line 31," *Speculum* 8:2 (1933): 195.

48 George L. Frost, "The Music of the Kinges Note," *Speculum* 8:2 (1933): 526–528.

49 *Reynold's Newspaper*, 24 Sept. 1893.

50 Howe, p. 186.

51 *Contemporary Review* 56 (July/Dec. 1898): 94–105.

52 *Magazine of Art* 2 (1888): 104.

53 *Bristol Mercury and Daily Post*, 11 Jan. 1890: iss. 13000.

54 Haweis, "More News of Chaucer," *Belgravia* 48 (1882): Pt. I, p. 45.

55 Ibid., 46.

56 Marion Harry Spielmann, "The Portraits of Geoffrey Chaucer," in *An Essay Written on the Occasion of the Quincentenary of the Poet's Death* (London: Kegan Paul, Trench, Trübner, 1900).

57 Haweis, "More News of Chaucer," 166.

58 Ibid., 164.

59 Ibid.

60 Robert K. Root, *The Poetry of Chaucer: A Guide to Its Study and Appreciation* (Boston: Houghton Mifflin, 1906), 214.

61 Derek Brewer, *Canterbury Tales*, Vol. 1, pt. 1 (London: Routledge, 1996), 182.

62 Erwin Panofsky, *Early Netherlandish Painting*, Vol. 1 (New York: Harper & Row, 1953), 161.

63 Haweis, "More News of Chaucer," 166.

64 *Lloyd's Weekly Newspaper*, 1 Aug. 1875: iss. 1706.

5 Finale

The National Home Reading Union

The National Home Reading Union which was inaugurated in Lord Aberdeen's drawing-room on Saturday may develop into the missing link which shall complete the moral and intellectual evolution of the rising generation.

Pall Mall Gazette, Monday, April 15, 1889, Iss. 7512

Only think of taking up a course of reading English literature up to the close of the Elizabethan epoch, and spending a few shillings only on such books as . . . Mrs. Haweis's *Chaucer for Schools*.

Anonymous, *Western Times*, Tuesday, August 5, 1890

In 1870 the Education Act in Britain mandated schooling of all children between the ages of five and twelve.[1] Since more children, hence, more adults, had now become literate, educators became increasingly aware not only of *what* was read but also *how* the material was assimilated, for a number of private surveys revealed that "the newly literate public preferred "*TitBits*[2] and *Pearson's Weekly* to literary fiction or educational writings."[3] The penny dreadful, also called a "blood," was "an inexpensive novel of violent adventure or crime that was especially popular in mid- to late-Victorian England; [it contained] rather careless and second-rate writing as well as gory themes,"[4] and it often claimed to be "historical."

The *Derby Daily Telegraph* announced on Saturday, February 1896 that "there was fear that more graphic novels and comics had a harmful influence of the behaviour of young women and boys, sometimes to the point of actually encouraging crime." It was necessary not only to direct the new readers of the elementary schools towards canonical texts but also to teach them how to read independently and reflectively and to induce a process of self-improvement based on recognition of externally prescribed standards."[5] "The gulf between the *Illustrated Police News* and Dante was too wide to contemplate" alone.[6] Thus the National Home Reading Union (NHRU) was born. And it is to this assembly that we owe our last glimpse of Chaucer scholar Mary Eliza Joy Haweis.

From its beginning the group endeavored to engage the *best* speakers (including the Rev. Haweis himself[7]), to host the *biggest* names, and to boast the most alluring topics. Lectures on botany, archaeology, and physical geography were set beside "Shakespeare on the French Stage," Gollancz's description of the Exeter Book, and the "Old Village Church." These talks were combined with tours of the various host cities, musical recitals, and exhibitions of "scientific novelties." Attendees might book for a week, a day, or a lecture. A point of pride was excellence of the rhetorical delivery. The Union (so it claimed) aimed for academic superiority by hiring those who could actually *teach*. A writer for the *Manchester Times* who signed her name as "Miriam" noted on Saturday, August 3, 1889, that

> lectures on all sorts of interesting subjects have been given by some of the cleverest lecturers in England, and the lecturers have taken pains to make their lectures pop and lively. Dry lectures, indeed, would have gone for to kill the scheme, instead of, as is now the case, arousing enthusiasm.

It is against this background that Mrs. Haweis wrote to her son Lionel on November 11, 1897: "Did I tell you that I have charge of the Chaucer course in the 'National Home Reading Union'?"

While the NHRU was an influential organization, advertised energetically though haphazardly in the local papers throughout its tenure, records of its activities seem to have been carelessly preserved, and archival materials are difficult to come by. Only the British Library (and possibly the Manchester Public Library) holds a complete run of journals. Apparently the "localized nature of the [reading] circles resulted in geographically scattered records" of a collection that was relatively scant to begin with.[8] By some small miracle, however, Haweis's materials remain intact.

The letter to her son about her Chaucer course came on the heels of brief letters from Alex Hill, chair of the Executive Committee of the NHRU and master of Downing College, Cambridge.[9] On August 1, 1897, Dr. Hill wrote on behalf of the group:

> Dear Mrs. Haweis
>
> The Committee of the NHRU have asked me to try to induce you to take charge of the first half of our English Lit course during the ensuring winter. It will be limited to Chaucer and the text-book Corson selections.
>
> You know our work and our members know well your Excellent edition of the Tales.
>
> Our ambition this winter will aim a little higher than it did when Chaucer was last in our cycle – some critical study of the language – history of the times – meter, etc. as well as the matter of the Tales. We should need four or five brief articles for the magazine – commencing in October & we [???] in return the normal remuneration of one guinea per article.
>
> I trust that we have sufficiently secured your sympathy to obtain your cooperation.
>
> Believe me Yours truly
> Alex Hill.

Haweis's response is not extant, but on August 4, 1897, Alex Hill wrote in confirmation of his offer:

> Dear Mrs. Haweis,
>
> I am very glad that you will write the articles – or some of the articles – for the Chaucer course for the NHRU. Our councilors advised us that your books on Chaucer handly [sic] fitted the course as planned this year – admirably as they had suited our members when we were dating Chaucer as only one of the XIV to VI Century poets.
>
> This time we propose to specialize on Chaucer [?], taking Hiram Corson's selections of the former poet as the textbook [?] study when language &c of Chaucer especially wh/in [?] times & circumstances in which he wrote.
>
> If you think that your book (?) 'Chaucer for School' should be in the "recommended" list I will gladly insert it.
>
> May we look for an introductory article (1600 words) by Sept. 15? Also *may I ask Prof Skeat for an article on say the English of Chaucer?* [emphasis mine] Had I been (?) coming to town just now I would have called to talk about the course – but time presses.
>
> > Believe me,
> > Yours very Truly,
> > Alex Hill

Even without Haweis's response, these brief letters yield considerable insight into the reputation that by 1897 she had gained as a writer. If Hill wanted Skeat's work, he *knew* had to ask permission from Mary Eliza to get it

Haweis's Chaucer texts had been on the NHRU's recommended book list since its inception, which explains "National Home Reading Union" stamped (after the fact) in gold on the front of an 1881 edition published by Chatto & Windus, Piccadilly. The text(s) had already been used successfully for past sessions. I have been unable to determine who taught Chaucer when the NHRU scheduled the early "Medieval Literature" course, but whoever it was, Haweis was considered superior, and the fact that Chaucer was allotted a course of his own was largely due to her scholarship and to her influence in popularizing the poet. In addition, Haweis's work, which covers much of the same material as *Selections from Chaucer's "Canterbury Tales,"* was recommended to go alongside Corson's.

Corson's take on teaching Chaucer is quite different from Haweis's. His book, published almost two decades after her *Chaucer for Children*,[10] contained only *The Nun's Priest's Tale* and *The Pardoner's Tale* in complete form, and various pieces – mostly exempla and character descriptions – from some of the other works. Corson was a professor at Cornell University and a recognized public lecturer on Milton, Browning, and Shakespeare, as well as on Chaucer. His lectures, according to the *Aberdeen Weekly Journal*, gave rise "to a number of Chaucer Clubs for the study of the poet. One, in Syracuse, [was] composed of German scholars, and ha[d] done good work."[11] Cornell had reluctantly admitted women students, but Corson pitched exclusively to intellectual men. He discusses Chaucer's metaphors and maxims but not Chaucer's puns, as though he were oblivious to any work that had been done on them. His explanatory notes make numerous references to the Chaucer Society, Furnivall, Skeat, Morris, and Lounsbury. There is nothing in his text to compare with Haweis's supplementary essays, her "Afterwards" and "Notes by the Way." With regard to the Union's guidelines, *Chaucer for Schools* was simply the "better" text, and Haweis knew it.

Buried in Professor Lounsbury's work is, of course, the reference to Mary Eliza Haweis and Thomas Chaucer, and Corson would have been aware of it. The considerable work she had done in archives, via scholarly documents, lurks beneath his phrase "a great deal of controversy" and it is dismissed accordingly.

Professor Corson could actually have taken a few rhetorical tips from Mary Eliza, for his text is deadly dull, a fact indicating that his book was a political and not a popular choice. After a brief biographical discussion, he builds his introduction around a series of tightly packed and tedious *lists*: Chaucer's similes, alliterations, allusions to the Bible, and "Synopses of Grammatical Forms." Submerged in his notes at the back of the text are certain engrossing nuggets, but these require considerable digging, and there is nothing like Haweis's lively preliminaries to the Pilgrims:

> And so it may be said, to get back to our poet [Corson had paused for a discussion of Milton], that *The Canterbury Tales* could hardly have been written by any one, the requisite poetical genius being given, who had not had the wide relationships and dealings with all sorts and conditions of men which Chaucer certainly had in the numerous positions in the civil service, which he filled, and in the diplomatic missions in which he bore a part.
>
> (p. xix)

Snooze.

To the contrary, Haweis had written,

> Some of Chaucer's best tales are not told by himself. They are put into the mouths of other people. In those days there were no newspapers – indeed there was not much news – so that when strangers who had little in common were thrown together, as they often were in inns, or in long journeys, they had few topics of conversation: and so they used to entertain each other by singing songs, or quite as often by telling their own adventures, or long stories such as Chaucer has written down and called the *Canterbury Tales*.
>
> (*CS*, p. 31)

Her audience has been primed.

It is not as though Corson did not know Mrs. Haweis personally; he did. Letters from the Cornell University archives confirm that Hugh Reginald wrote to Dr. Corson with some regularity, asking that paid lectures be set up for the reverend whenever he might be in the vicinity of Ithaca. Although one might assume that correspondence had taken place between Mary Eliza and Professor Corson regarding the course itself, none is preserved in this archive. There is, however, one letter written to Mrs. Corson by Mrs. Haweis, on February 3, 1887, where the latter anticipates the Corson's spring visit to England. She says, "I do hope . . . that we shall see much more of you than when you were last here." Then, casually dismissing her own work in a self-deprecating way that could not have been sincere, she adds that she is sending along her *Tales from Chaucer*:

> A young friend, daughter of Mrs. Justin McCarttey who is lecturing in the States, is going to post you a tiny book of mine (Chaucer paraphrased) which is hardly worth Prof. Corson's glance, but will just serve to show that old Chaucer is not dead in all hearts, since there has been a call for this, in a cheap "People's Library" that my husband has been editing for some time with unparalleled success.

There is no surviving response. But perhaps what we don't know about any conversations, letters, decisions, prearrangements, and understandings between Mary Eliza and the Corsons is ancillary to what we *do* know: Haweis had little respect for Corson's work; she *was* invited to take charge of the Chaucer course, and she *did* agree to write articles for the magazines. Apparently, Corson was not asked, or, at least, there is no evidence to the contrary. Both *Chaucer for Schools* and *Tales from Chaucer* were mainstays on the list of the group's suggested readings. As the Union grew, so did the students who would clearly have been exposed to Haweis's theories. By the process of osmosis her ideas became a part of the Chaucer reserve, invisible as air, but attendant nonetheless.

In his second letter to Haweis, Hill had asked permission to secure an article by W. W. Skeat, arguably the most recognized Chaucerian of his time, on "Chaucer's English," from a woman whose own fame seems to have been spotty at best. If the article were written, it is not included in the course materials. The only other extant records of this Chaucer course or the one that preceded it, are Haweis's own articles written for the *National Home-Reading Union Magazine*. Haweis published five articles under the heading of "English Literature": "Chaucer" (October, 1897); "Christian Astrology in Chaucer" (November, 1897); "Chaucer's Education" (February, 1898); "Chaucer" (March, 1898); and "Chaucer's Music" (May, 1898). These are all solid essays, and although she rehashes some of her earlier material, she adds much that is new, and she adds it with considerable aplomb.

Haweis begins with a general introduction to the poet and his methodology. Chaucer is more subtle than Milton or Shakespeare and his characters take more careful probing.

> Chaucer remodeled and enriched, with astonishing dexterity, the vernacular, then a *congeries* of harsh dialects differing as widely as Venetian and roman *patois* to-day; and made it a precise, expressive, and even harmonious vehicle of thought – nay, he could play with it, introducing meter, *motifs à trios étages*. . . . and minute analyses of human character.

For Shakespeare and Milton, the language was "ready made." Haweis believed that Chaucer's work was performed orally, and in an idea she credited to herself

("It has never, I think, been pointed out.") noted "how completely the thrust of many of Chaucer's sentences may be reversed by change of accent and facial expression in reading." The poet knew that *The Canterbury Tales* would be read to a variety of audiences with widely contrasting ideologies and that the work would be discussed and disseminated to the "rasping or prodigal monarch, the servile court-man, the 'double' wife, the foolish old man in the hands of an unprincipled girl," and on and on. Chaucer's carefully crafted style, his exact word placement, and his application of richly nuanced words allowed him infinite freedom of meaning. Should he worry about libel? Probably not. Although scribes produced many copies of the *Tales*, presumably for vastly different audiences, Chaucerians mostly associate a "reading" with the early fifteenth-century "*Troilus* Frontispiece" where the poet himself reads to a group of elegantly clad lords and ladies. There is a castle in the background. When Chaucer's works are viewed against such a backdrop, certain scenes and motifs are necessarily foregrounded, and although scholars know this picture is not an accurate rendering, still it is the one that comes most readily to mind.

But Haweis postulates another scenario. Harry Bailly

> was a citizen doubtless as well-known as Chaucer himself. . . . and until ten years ago the Tabard Inn was still standing, and I sketched it during the demolition. . . . This celebrated inn was the general and very necessary rendezvous, and starting point for all travelers riding southward, or returning thence.

Might not the work have been performed there? Chaucer seems to have had almost limitless knowledge of the court and its activities, but he was also heavily involved in the transactions of the middle class. In my book *Chaucer's "Legal Fiction,"*[12] I find Chaucer to have been acutely aware of mercantile laws, even seemingly obscure ones, that would have affected those who might have gathered at the Tabard, and that it formed a part both of his vocabulary and of his story line. Haweis does not carry this further, but it was as clear to her, as it is to modern audiences, that what Chaucer is "about" depends on just who has the book in hand.

As one who was married to a musician for most of her life, it is not surprising that Mary Eliza's final essay for the NHRU was "Chaucer's Music." But what *is* surprising is the different approach she took from her husband who had written of music and morals and of old violins. Earlier, in *Chaucer for Schools*, she had mentioned quavers and crockets but here she goes so far as to suggest a relationship between Chaucer's iambic meter – "the smoothness of his melodious verse" – and the alternating voices of counterpoint. Haweis relies heavily on John Hullah's book *The History of Modern Music*, and as Hullah refers to the secular music of the Squire, the Miller, the Pardoner, the Sumptnour [sic] and the Host "to which the world is indebted," so, too, does she. Hullah observes that

> Musical composition does not consist in an unintermittent [sic] presentation of new thoughts, but in the development, the pursuit to their ultimate consequences of a few thoughts, even of a single one; technically in making the

same passage heard successively in various scales, in various parts, and under various forms of accompaniment.[13]

Such has been Haweis's understanding of Chaucer's technique as she has illustrated over and again in her "Notes by the Way" and especially in her discussions of *The Miller's Tale*. This would be Mary Eliza's last essay, and she carried the thesis no further. Nor can I find a modern writer who has done so, but John P. McCall comes close in 1970 when, in discussing the critical perplexity of *The Parliament of Foules*, he notes that perhaps

> we have been looking and listening for the wrong things. It would seem, for example, that criticism has expected of the poem one or another kind of linear unity leading to a hidden answer, a reconciliation or a resolution; but what the Parliament has and abundantly depicts is an interweaving of conflicting elements that are held together in concord and balance. To put it another way, we seem to have been listening for the monophonic sound of Georgian chant when, in fact, the poem sings to us in counterpoint and polyphone.[14]

It is difficult to believe that Mary Eliza Joy Haweis would not have agreed.

On October 23, 1898, *Lloyd's Weekly Newspaper* observed that

> an interesting course of free lectures for the people is "Glimpses of English literature." . . . arranged by F. Herbert Stead to be held in the hall, York-Street, Walworth, on Tuesday evenings. The first lecture will be given next Thursday by Dr. F. J. Furnivall, M.A., on "Old English Poetry," when Dr. Macnamara will preside: on Nov. 3, Mrs. Haweis will lecture on the Canterbury Pilgrims.

Mary Eliza never gave this lecture. Somewhere around that time, in "delicate health," she had been moved to Bath, where she died on November 24, possibly from complications caused by kidney failure.

Bea Howe's notoriously unreliable biography of Haweis's life ends with an impassioned "scene" from Haweis's final days:

> She insisted on leaving her bed to sit by the window. Every now and then her tired eyes kept turning to a large poster that hung from the end of her bed. The poster announced her appearance at the Browning Hall, Walworth, where she had promised Mr. W. T. Stead [sic] to give a talk on Chaucer to a society of Working Men in which he was interested. That she might not be able to fulfill this promise was preying on her mind.
>
> On her husband's next visit she asked him what she could do in regard to her Chaucer lecture. When he promised that he might do it for her she accepted his offer gratefully. There and then, they got out the box of coloured glass slides which she had made as illustrations from the chromo-lithographs for her book *Chaucer for Children*. Amicably, they made notes together. . . .

The following afternoon he gave his wife's talk on Chaucer at Walworth which was extremely successful.[15]

There is no reason to doubt that he did give the talk, but these scenes cannot be verified. We do know, however, that his wife had cut him off without a cent and that he knew it and spent her last days vainly and frantically trying to change her mind.

Mary Eliza Haweis devoted much of her brief life to an understanding of Chaucer, and contemporary assessments of late nineteenth-century Chaucer texts prove instructive with regard to an acknowledgment of her life's work. In 1898, the year that Haweis died, James M. Garnett reviewed "recent" Chaucer books for the *American Journal of Philology*: two works by Skeat, one by Lounsbury, and another by Alfred W. Pollard, et al. Skeat had completed the last of his six-volume series with a supplementary volume entitled "Chaucerian and Other Pieces," and Garnett proclaimed with authority that "Prof. Skeat has now placed all students of Chaucer under increased obligations by the completion of the Oxford edition." Skeat had also "edited the complete works of Chaucer in one volume, as 'The Student's Chaucer,' being the text of the Oxford edition. With Pollard's text and the three volumes of Lounsbury's 'Studies in Chaucer,' it is difficult to see what more the student of Chaucer could desire."[16] In 1894, O. B. Rhodes's review of Pollard's 1893 *Primer* applauds Pollard for his "thoroughness and sanity of criticism,"[17] which confirms "Matthew Arnold's prophecy: "Today Chaucer has more readers and more lovers that [sic] at any previous time and every year increases their number."[18] Rhodes praises Saunders' "Canterbury Tales" and observes that

> With the help of Pollard's Primer and 'Saunders' Canterbury Tales,' the charm of this art may well win its way into a course of instruction in English literature in our best secondary schools. *For the teacher at least, Chaucer need no longer stand a stranger at the door.*
>
> (emphasis mine)

Writers penned numerous obituaries about Haweis, but none, I believe, that Mary Eliza would applaud. She was acclaimed as superintendent of the Mercy (Animals) Branch of the British Woman's Temperance Association, a "strong supporter of the woman's franchise movement," and "was a member of the Committee of the Central and Western Society." She was "her husband's companion in many of his foreign travels, and illustrated some of his books." She wrote *The Art of Beauty*, the *Art of Decoration*, and *The Art of Dress*. She *also* wrote books on Chaucer. So far as I can determine, only one American newspaper, the *New York Times*, noted that she was "Directoress of the Chaucer Course in the National Home Reading Union, Surrey House, Victorian Embankment" (November 29, 1898, n.p.). The remainder either didn't know or didn't care.

Gone today are the conversations from the Reading Room, the viewing of manuscripts unloaded from carts and the repositories filling with parchment and various gelatinous materials; silent are the jokes about heron's heads and complaints about too few aides to carry materials to eager researchers. Walter Rye's discourses on the Rolls Series have quieted, and Deutsch has faded away, inhaling too much smut and soil from the dank and overcrowded library shelves. And Mary Eliza Haweis, whose diligence and action, whose originality and creativity would come almost to naught, has receded into an occasional antique bookstore and junk shop. But *her* Chaucer echoes in unexpected places, in books and articles, conference papers and classroom lectures. The close readings she insisted on, the archival materials necessary for support, are at the heart of Chaucer scholarship today. Her belief that there "is so much hidden in Chaucer that we can never get it all," is now an apothegm. The first to discover puns, the first to uncover portraits, the first true interdisciplinary Chaucer scholar. . . . As Maitland had eulogized Mary Bateson in 1906, "I do not know the man who both could and would have done so much and done so well."

Notes

1 *Examiner*, 20 Aug 1870: iss. 3264. For the provisions of this Act, see Great Britain Laws, Statutes, etc. *Elementary Act, 1870. Bristol Selected Pamphlets*. See also James Murphy, "Educational Act of 1870, Text and Commentary," *Journal of Educational Studies* 20:3 (Oct. 1972): 345–346.
2 For information on the TitBits, see Joseph A. Dane and Alexandra Gillespie. "Back at Chaucer's Tomb: Chaucer's 'Workes'," *Digital Victorian*, Dr. Bob Richardson Research Blog. bobnicholson@edgehill.ac.uk (5/18/2014).
3 *Pearson's Weekly* seems to have been more respectable. In 1901, the *New York Times* noted that its "increasing circulation . . . cannot be due to anything else than the good judgment shown in the selection of the material to be found in the magazine" (Nov. 23, 1901), http://onlinebooks.library.upenn.edu/webbin/serial?id=pearsonsusa.
4 Robert Snape, "The National Home Reading Union," *Journal of Victorian Culture* 7 (Spring 2002): 87.
5 Ibid.
6 Ibid.
7 For the very first session, the room for "Music and Morals" was filled to overcrowding and this same lecture was repeated in 1894 by request (*Manchester Times*, 27 July 1889).
8 Felicity Stimpson, "Reading in Circles: The National Home Reading Union, 1889–1900," *Publishing History* 52 (2002): 67n4. See also Robert Snape, *Leisure and the Rise of the Public Library* (London: Library Association, 1995), 119.
9 UBC, Box H-28.
10 Hiram Corson, *Chaucer's Canterbury Tales* (New York: Macmillan, 1896).
11 *Aberdeen Weekly Journal*, 26 July 1893.
12 Mary Flowers Braswell, *The Medieval Sinner* (East Brunswick, NJ: Associated University Press, 2001).
13 Hullah (1875; rpt; London: Longman's Green, 1896), 44.
14 John P. McCall, "The Harmony of Chaucer's Parliament," *Chaucer Review* 5:1 (Summer 1970): 22–31.
15 *School Review* 9:4 (1898): 439–445.
16 Ibid., 279.
17 Ibid., 277.
18 Ibid., 439–445.

Select bibliography

Books, pamphlets, and journal articles

Adam, Madame, Rev. H. Adler, Walter Besant, et al. "The Tree of Knowledge," *New Review* 10 (1894): 675–690.

Akbari, Suzanne Conklin. *Seeing through the Veil: Optical Theory & Medieval Allegory*. Toronto: Toronto University Press, 2005.

Altick, Richard D. *The English Common Reader: A Social History of the Mass Reading Public 1800–1900*. Athens: Ohio University Press, 2nd ed., 1998.

Anger, Suzy. *Victorian Interpretations*. Ithaca, NY: Cornell University Press, 2005.

Anonymous. "The Song of Chaucer's Clerk of Oxenford, 'Angelus ad Virginem,'" *Month* 44 (1882): 100–102.

Baedeker's Great Britain: Handbook for Travelers. Koblance: Leipsic, 1890.

Barrington, Candace. "'Forget What You Have Learned': The Mistick Krewe's 1914 Mardi Gras Chaucer," *American Literary History* 22:4 (2010): 806–830.

Baum, Paul. "Chaucer's Puns," *PMLA* 71:1 (Mar. 1956): 225–246.

Beichner, Paul E. "Characterization in *The Miller's Tale*," in *Chaucer Criticism, I: The Canterbury Tales: An Anthology*, pp. 117–129. Eds. Richard J. Schoeck and Jerome Taylor. Notre Dame: University of Notre Dame Press, rpt. 1960.

Bell, Robert. Ed. *Poetical Works of Geoffrey Chaucer*, Vol. 1. London: John Parker and Son, 1855.

Bellamy, Joan, Anne Laurence, and Gillian Perry, Eds. *Women, Scholarship and Criticism: Gender and Knowledge, c. 1790–1900*. Manchester: Manchester University Press, 2003.

Benson, Larry. Gen Ed. *The Riverside Chaucer*. Boston: Houghton Mifflin, 1987.

Benzie, William. *Dr. F. J. Furnivall: Victorian Scholar Adventurer*. Norman, OK: Pilgrim Books, 1983.

Bond, Edward. "New Facts in the Life of Geoffrey Chaucer," *Fortnightly Review* 6 (1866): 28–29.

Bradfield, Thomas. "A Dominant Note in Some Recent Fiction," *Westminster Review* 142 (1985): 537–545.

Braswell, Mary Flowers. *Chaucer's 'Legal Fiction'*. East Brunswick, NJ: Associated University Press, 2001.

Brewer, Derek. "Modernizing the Medieval: Eighteenth-Century Translations of Chaucer," in *The Middle Ages after the Middle Ages in the English-Speaking World*, pp. 103–120. Eds. Marie Françoise Alamichel and Derek Brewer. Cambridge: Brewer, 1997.

Brown, Peter. *Chaucer and the Making of Optical Space*. New York: Peter Lang, 2007.

Burgin, G. B. "Some British Museum Stories: A Chat with Dr. Garnett," *Ideler* 5 (July 1894): 370–337.

Burke, Ulick Ralph. *Sancho Panza's Proverbs & Others Which Occur in Don Quixote.* London: Pickering & Chatto, 2nd ed., 1877.

Carrington, Evelyn. *Folk-Lore Record* 2 (1878): 127–134.

CCH. "Notes on Dress," *Art Amateur: A Monthly Journal Devoted to Art in the Household (1879–1903)* (Apr. 1882): 108.

Chance, Jane, Ed. *Medievalists and the Academy.* Madison: University of Wisconsin Press, 2004.

Clarke, Charles Cowden. Ed. *The Riches of Chaucer.* 1835; 2nd ed.; rpt. London: Heritage Press, 1870.

———. *Tales from Chaucer Told for Young People in Which His Impurities Have Been Expunged.* 1833; 2nd ed., 1870; rpt. London: Heritage Press, 1952.

Collins, Fletcher. "*The Miller's Tale*, Line 31," *Speculum* 8:2 (1933): 195–197.

Corson, Hiram. *Chaucer's Canterbury Tales.* New York: Macmillan, 1896.

Crakantorpe, B. A. "Sex in Modern Literature," *Nineteenth Century* 37 (1985): 607–616.

Crane, David. "A Test of the Invisible College," *American Sociological Review* (1969): 335–352.

Cunningham, Colin. "Hints on Household Taste and the Art of Decoration: Authors, Their Audiences and Gender in Interior Design," in *Women Scholarship and Criticism*, pp. 159–187. Eds. Joan Bellamy, Anne Laurence, and Gillian Perry. Manchester: Manchester University Press, 2001.

Dane, Joseph A. *Who Is Buried in Chaucer's Tomb?* East Lansing: Michigan State University Press, 1988.

——— and Alexandra Gillespie. "Back at Chaucer's Tomb: Chaucer's 'Workes'," Studies in Bibliography 52 (1999).

Echard, Siân. *Printing in the Middle Ages.* Philadelphia: University of Pennsylvania Press, 2008.

Ellis, Alexander. *Early English Pronunciation.* EETS, ES, 14. London: Trübner, 1896.

Ellis, Steve. *Chaucer at Large.* Minneapolis: University of Minnesota Press, 2001.

Fisher, Judith L. and Mark Allen. "Victorian Illustrations to Chaucer's *Canterbury Tales*," in *Chaucer Illustrated*, pp. 233–273. Eds. William K. Finley and Judith Rosenbaum. London: British Library, 2003.

Fleay, F. G. "Some Folklore of Chaucer," *Folk-lore Record* 2 (1879): 136–142.

Frost, George L. "The Music of the Kinges Note," *Speculum* 8 (1933): 526–528.

Furnivall, F. J. "Recent Work on Chaucer," *Macmillan's Magazine* 27 (1873): 383–393.

Haas, Renate. "Caroline F. E. Spurgeon (1869–1942): The First Woman Professor in England," in *Women Medievalists and the Academy*, pp. 102–103. Ed. Jane Chance. Madison: University of Wisconsin Press, 2004.

Haber, Rev. John. "*The Canterbury Tales of Geoffrey Chaucer*," *College English* 11:1 (1949): 53–54.

Hales, John W. *Notes and Essays on Shakespeare.* London: G. Bell & Sons, 1884.

Hannigan, D. F. "Sex in Fiction," *Westminster Review* 142 (1985): 616–625.

Hartshorne, C. H. *The Book of Rarities in the University of Cambridge, Illustrated by Original Letters and Notes, Biographical, Literary, and Antiquarian.* London: Longman, 1829.

Haweis, H. R. "Tales from Chaucer" (Introduction to series), in *The Canterbury Tales of Chaucer, Completed in a Modern Version*, 3 vols. Ed. Hugh Reginald Lipscomb. London: J. Cooke, 1887.

———. "Words for Women," quoted by Bea Howe, in *Arbiter of Elegance*. London: Harvill Press, 1967.

Haweis, Mary Eliza. "Afterwards: The Miller's Tale," *Tales from Chaucer*, (1887): p. 64. Ed. H. R. Haweis. London: George Routledge & Sons.

———. *Chaucer for Children*. London: Chatto & Windus, 1877.

———. *Chaucer for Schools*. London: Chatto & Windus, 1881.

———. "Chaucer's Characters," *University Magazine* 93:3 (1879): 26–40.

———. "Equality of the Sexes," *Review of Reviews* 4 (1873).

———. "Insanity Considered as a Plea for Divorce," *Review of Reviews* 18 (Feb. 1898): 174.

———. "Married Woman's Property Act," *Spectator Archive* 24 (Mar. 1883): 25.

———. "More News of Geoffrey Chaucer," *Belgravia* 48 (1882): Pt. I, 34–46.

———. "More News of Geoffrey Chaucer," *Belgravia* 4 (1882): Pt. II, 160–172.

———. "The Wife's Private Purse," *Women at Home* 4 (1895): 455.

———. "Young Wives and Their Difficulties," *Young Woman* 4 (Sept. 1896): 417.

Hempl, Rev. George. "Chaucer's Canterbury Tales," *MLN* 10:3 (Mar. 1895): 180.

Hill, Thomas E. *The Essential Handbook of Victorian Etiquette* (1873–1890); rpt. San Francisco: Bluewood Books, 1994.

Holberg, Jennifer and Marcy H. Taylor. "Pedagogy: Cultural Approaches to Teaching Literature and Language," *Composition and Culture* 4:1 (2004): 29.

Holley, Linda Tarte. "Medieval Optics and the Framed Narrative in Chaucer's 'Troilus and Criseyde'," *Chaucer Review* 21 (1986): 26–44.

Honig, Edith Lazaros. *Breaking the Angelic Image*. New York: Greenwood Press, 1988.

Hudson, Roger. Introduction to *A Short History of the English People*, pp. xiii–xxii, by John Richard Green. 1874; rpt. London: Folio Society, 1992.

Hunter, Joseph. "The Seal of Chaucer: Copy of the Deed to Which Is Appended: Copy of Public Instrument Notifying to Him His Removal from His Office of Clerk of the King's Works," *Archaeologia* 34 (1852): 42–45.

Jamieson, Anna. *Memoirs of the Loves of the Poets*. Boston: Ticknor and Fields, 1844.

Kittredge, George Lyman. *Chaucer and His Poetry*. Cambridge: Harvard University Press, 1914; rpt. 1946.

Lambarde, William. *Dictionarium Angliae Topograph & Historicam*. Boston: Ticknor & Fields, 1730.

Laurence, Anne, Joan Bellamy and Gillian Perry. Eds. *Women, Scholarship, and Criticism*. Manchester: Manchester University Press, 2003.

Levine, Philippa. *The Amateur and the Professional*. London: Cambridge University Press, 1986.

Lipscomb, William. Ed. *The Canterbury Tales of Chaucer, Completed in a Modern Version*, Vol. 1. London: J. Cooke, & G . . . & J. Robinson, Oxford, 1795.

Lucas, Angela. "The Mirror in the Marketplace: Januarie through the Looking Glass," *Chaucer Review* 33 (1998): 123–145.

Manly, John. "Three Recent Chaucer Studies," *Review of English Studies* 10:30 (1934): 262.

Matthews, David. *The Making of Middle English, 1765–1910*. Minneapolis: University of Minnesota Press, 1999.

Maura, Ives. "'The Summit of the Author's Fame': Victorian Women Writers and the Birthday Book," in *Women Writers and the Artifacts of Celebrity in the Long Nineteenth Century*, pp. 95–118. Eds. Ann R. Hawkins and Maura Ives. Burlington: Ashgate, 2012.

McCall, John P. "The Harmony of Chaucer's Parliament," *Chaucer Review* 5:1 (Summer 1970): 22–31.

Melrose, Robin and Diana Gardner. "The Language of Control in Victorian Children's Literature," in *Victorian Identities: Social and Cultural Formations in Nineteenth-Century Literature*. Eds. Ruth Robbins and Julia Wolfrey. New York: Palgrave Macmillan, 1996.

Miller, Mary Dockray. "Mary Bateson (1865–1906): Scholar and Suffragist," in *Women Medievalists and the Academy*, pp. 67–78. Ed. Jane Chance. Madison: University of Wisconsin Press, 2004.

Miller, Miriam. "Illustrations of the *Canterbury Tales* for Children: A Mirror of Chaucer's World," *Chaucer Review* 27:3 (1993): 293–304.

Minto, William. *Characteristics of English Poets from Chaucer to Shirley*. Edinburgh: Blackwood & Sons, 1874.

Morley, Henry. *First Sketch of English Literature in the Nineteenth Century*. London: Cassel, 1873.

Morse, Charlotte C. "Popularizing Chaucer in the Nineteenth Century," *Chaucer Review* 38 (2003): 99–125.

Murphy, James. "Educational Act of 1870, Text and Commentary," *Journal of Educational Studies* 20:3 (Oct. 1972): 345–346.

Muscatine, Charles. *Chaucer and the French Tradition*. Berkeley: University of California Press, 1957.

Panofsky, Erwin. *Early Netherlandish Painting*. Vol. 1. New York: Harper & Row, 1953.

Patch, Howard. "A Commentary on the General Prologue of the *Canterbury Tales* of Geoffrey Chaucer," *Modern Language Notes* 64:7 (1949): 64–66.

Pendergast, Thomas A. *Chaucer's Dead Body*. New York: Routledge, 2004.

Phegley, Jennifer. *Educating the Proper Woman Reader*. Columbus: Ohio State University Press, 2004.

Reed, Rev. A. W. "Some New Light on Chaucer," *RES* 4 (1928): 217.

Richmond, Velma Bourgeois. *Chaucer as Children's Literature*. Jefferson, NC: McFarland, 2005.

Rock, Daniel. "The Paternity of Christian Doctrine – Chaucer's Night Charm," *Notes and Queries* (1850): 281.

Root, Robert K. *Poetry of Chaucer: A Guide to Its Study and Appreciation*. Boston: Houghton Mifflin, 1906.

Ross, W. Thomas. "Notes on Chaucer's *Miller's Tale*, A. 3216 & 3320," *English Language Notes* 13 (1976): 256–258.

Royster, Rev. James F. "Some New Light on Chaucer," *MLN* 42:4 (1927): 251.

Ruggiers, Paul G. *Editing Chaucer: The Great Tradition*. Norman, OK: Pilgrim Books, 1984.

Rye, Walter. *Records and Record Searching*. London: E. Stock, 1888.

Sanborn, Kate. "One View of Chaucer Mania," *Manhattan* 3 (1883): 307.

"Saturday Review on Chaucer's *Canterbury Tales*," *Academy* (Feb. 1874): 174.

Saunders, John. *Cabinet Pictures of English Life*. London: Charles Knight, 1841.

Sawyer, Robert. "Furnivall and the Scientific Method," Vol II, no 2, Fall/Winter 2006, Christy Desmet and Sujata Iyengar Eds, Borrowers and Lenders: The Journal of Shakespeare and Appropriation is supported by the University of Georgia English Department, http://borrowers.uga.edu/781463/show#subtitle1

Selby, W. D. *The Life Records of Chaucer*. London: Kegan Paul, Trench, Trübner, 1875.

Simon, Hugo. "Chaucer as a Wicliffite: An Essay on Chaucer's Parson and *Parson's Tale*," *Chaucer Society Essays* I (1876): 232–243.

Skeat, Walter W. Ed. *The Complete Works of Chaucer*, 6 Vols. Oxford, 1894.

———. *Early English Proverbs: Chiefly of the Thirteenth and Fourteenth Centuries, with Illustrative Quotations*. Oxford: Clarendon Press, 1910.

Smith, Bonnie G. *The Gender of History*. Cambridge: Cambridge University Press, 1995.

Snape, Robert. *Leisure and the Rise of the Public Library*. London: Library Association, 1995.

———. "The National Home Reading Union," *Journal of Victorian Culture* 7 (Spring 2002): 87–93.

Snoad, Warner. "A Voice from the Talmud," *Woman's Herald* 2:77 (1893).

Spielmann, Marion Harry. "The Portraits of Geoffrey Chaucer," in *An Essay Written on the Occasion of the Quincentenary of the Poet's Death*. London: Kegan Paul, Trench, Trübner, 1900.

Stevens, John. *"Angelus ad Virginem*: The History of a Medieval Song," in *Medieval Studies for J.A.W. Bennett*, pp. 297–328. Ed. P.L. Heyworth. Oxford: Aetates S LXX, 1981.

Storr, Francis. *Canterbury Chimes*. London: Kegan Paul, 1898.

———. "Teaching of English Composition," *Educational Times* 50 (May 1897): 221.

Strohm, Paul. *Social Chaucer*. Cambridge: Harvard University Press, 1989.

Tatlock, John S. "Introduction," in *A Concordance to the Complete Works of Geoffrey Chaucer*. Gloucester, MA: Peter Smith, 1963; rpt. 1927, p. xi.

———. "Puns in Chaucer," in *Flugel Memorial Volume*, pp. 228–232. Stanford, CA: Stanford University, 1916.

Taylor, Mark. "Coloured Houses: Transgressing the Limits of the Domestic Realm," in *Limits: Proceedings from the 21st Annual Conference of the Society of Architectural Historians*. Eds. Harriet Edquest and Hélène Frichot (Australia & New Zealand: RMIT University, 2012).

Thoms, William. "Chaucer's Night Spell," *Folklore Record* 1 (1878): 145–154.

Trigg, Stephanie. *Congenial Souls*. Minneapolis: University of Minnesota Press, 2002.

Turner, Mark W. "Time, Periodicals, and Literary Studies," *Victorian Periodicals Review* 39:4 (2006).

Tyrwhitt, Thomas. *The Poetical Works of Chaucer*. London: Edward Moxon, 1852.

Urry, John, Ed. *Works of Geoffrey Chaucer*. London: Bernard Litten, 1721.

Whiting, Barlett Jere. *Chaucer's Use of Proverbs*. Cambridge: Harvard University Press, 1934.

Whiting, Rev. B.J. *Three Chaucer Studies*, by Russell Krauss, Haldeen Braddy and C. Robert Case. New York: Oxford University Press, 1932.

Willibald Hæckel's Das Sprichwort bei Chaucer. Vol. 8. Erlanger: Bertrage zur Englischen Philologie, 1890.

Wordsworth, Dorothy. *Journals of Dorothy Wordsworth*. Ed. E. De Sellingcourt, 2 Vols. (Entry for Saturday, December 26, 1801). London (1952), pp. 1–96.

Archival resources

Clipping in UBC Sous Fonds; Biographical Miscell MEH 2a, Folder 3, Box 31, n.p.

Furnivall Collected Papers, King's College.

Haweis Family Sous Fonds MEH Box 1, Misc. Box 31 (UBC).

Haweis's manuscript notes on the paintings for *Chaucer for Children* include the following sources: Vide MS. Reg 2 B. viii, and MS Imp. Lib. Paris, No. 7210, & etc., for "Dinner in the Olden Time"; Froissart's Chronicle, No. 2644, Bibl. Imp. De Paris, for "Lady Crossing Street"; Brit. Mus. Harl MS 4866 for the portrait of C; Royal Coll. 20 B.6; for the woodcuts; Royal Coll. 20 B.6; for the woodcuts: John of Gaunt; Royal MS, 14E. 4, temp. ED IV for the Monk ("too late"): the Doctor, Sloane Coll. No. 1975.

"Letter to her Mother," UBC Sous Fonds, 22–5.

MEH 30/15 "The Story of Alison."

Nolcken, C. von. University of British Columbia (UBC) Sous Fonds, Box 23, Folder 4–5.

Newspaper articles

Birmingham Daily Post, 28 Dec. 1874.
Birmingham Daily Post, 17 Jan. 1882.
Daily News, 6 Nov. 1876.
Examiner, 12 Feb. 1881.
Glasgow Herald, 20 June 1872: iss. 1002.
Glasgow Herald, 13 Nov. 1886, p. 272.
Graphic, 2 Dec. 1876: iss. 366.
Graphic, 3 Apr. 1880.
"The Ladies Column," *Manchester Times*, 27 Jan. 1877.
Leeds Mercury, 29 Nov. 1867: iss. 12056.
Leeds Mercury, 14 Mar. 1872: iss. 10585.
Leeds Mercury, 30 Jan. 1878: iss. 12420.
Leeds Mercury, 4 Aug. 1880.
Leeds Mercury, 27 Feb. 1897: iss. 12444.
Literary World, 28 Aug. 1880, p. 298.
Lloyd's Weekly Newspaper, 10 Dec. 1863.
London Daily News, 11 Jan. 1890.
Manchester Times, 30 Sept. 1876.
Morning Chronicle, 31 May 1850, p. 2065.
New York Times, 9 Jan. 1881.
Penny Illustrated Paper, 26 Dec. 1863, p. 422.
Reynold's Newspaper, 24 Sept. 1893: iss. 14.
Saturday Review, 14 Feb. 1874, p. 149.
Trewman's Exeter Flying Post, 27 Jan. 1875: iss. 5746.

Index

For Product Safety Concerns and Information please contact our EU
representative GPSR@taylorandfrancis.com
Taylor & Francis Verlag GmbH, Kaufingerstraße 24, 80331 München, Germany

www.ingramcontent.com/pod-product-compliance
Ingram Content Group UK Ltd.
Pitfield, Milton Keynes, MK11 3LW, UK
UKHW020946180425
457613UK00019B/541

*9 780367 880910 *